Rhythm, Riffs & Lead
How to Play
Rock

Michael Heatley, Alan Brown,
Myrddin Young & Leon Gruszecki

D1607194

FLAME TREE
PUBLISHING

Publisher and Creative Director: Nick Wells
Project Editor: Sara Robson
Music Composition: Myrddin Young and Leon Gruszecki
Guitars and Consultant: Jake Jackson
New Photography: Stephen Feather
Art Director: Mike Spender
Digital Design and Production: Chris Herbert
Layout Design: Jake

Special thanks to Cat Emslie, Claire Walker and Polly Willis

08 10 12 11 09
1 3 5 7 9 10 8 6 4 2

This edition first published 2008 by
FLAME TREE PUBLISHING
Crabtree Hall, Crabtree Lane
Fulham, London SW6 6TY
United Kingdom

www.flametreepublishing.com

Flame Tree Publishing is part of the Foundry Creative Media Co. Ltd

© 2008 this edition The Foundry Creative Media Co. Ltd

ISBN 978-1-84786-233-4

A CIP record for this book is available from the British
Library upon request.

Acknowledgements
All photographs and notation courtesy of Foundry Arts, except the following:
Boss: 53; Dorling Kindersley: 25; Getty Images/Michael Ochs Archive 10;
Redferns and the following photographers: Richard E. Aaron 373,
Chuck Boyd 14, Fin Costello 17, Ross Gilmore 381, Andrew Putler 9,
Simon Ritter: 377, S & G Press Agency 369, Robert Verhorst 13.

Michael Heatley (text) has written over 100 books, penned liner notes
to more than 100 CD reissues and written for magazines including *Music
Week*, *Billboard*, *Goldmine*, *Radio Times* and *Record Collector*. More recently
he was the author of *How to Write Great Songs* and *How To Play Hard, Metal
& Nu Rock* also published by Flame Tree.

Alan Brown (musical examples) is a former member of the Scottish National
Orchestra. Alan now works as a freelance musician, with several leading UK
orchestras, and as a consultant in music and IT. Alan has had several compositions
published, developed a set of music theory CD-Roms, co-written a series of Bass
Guitar Examination Handbooks and worked on over 100 further titles.

Printed in India

Contents

A Short History of Rock 368

Further Reading & Internet Sites 384

Key Terms

ARPEGGIO A broken chord in which the notes are played in succession rather than simultaneously (*see* page 30).

DISTORTION Distorted, harsh or fuzzy sounds created either accidentally or deliberately through overdriven amplification or distortion pedals (*see* page 50).

DOUBLE-STOP A technique involving playing two separate strings that are 'stopped' or depressed by the fingers and plucked simultaneously (*see* pages 17 & 40).

FEEDBACK The 'ringing' or 'howling' sound produced when pickups or microphones pick up the sound they produce through loudspeakers and feed it back, creating a sound loop.

HAMMER-ON A technique involving placing another finger forcefully onto the same string at a higher fret than the one first played in order to achieve a smooth sound (*see* pages 38–39).

LEGATO A technique involving playing notes in smooth succession, with no silent intervals, usually with 'hammer-ons' and 'pull-offs' (*see* page 48).

LICK A short phase or series of notes used as single-note melodic lines or solos (*see* page 15).

OPEN TUNING One where the strings are tuned so that a chord is achieved without fretting any of the strings (*see* pages 27 & 36).

OVERDRIVE A form of usually deliberate guitar distortion produced by running the amplifiers at overly high volume so that a 'growl' or 'edge' can be heard (*see* pages 26 & 47–50).

PALM MUTING A technique in which the side of the picking hand is placed across the strings close to the bridge to stop the strings vibrating when they are plucked (*see* pages 41 & 48–49).

PICKUP A device, usually mounted on the body of the guitar underneath the strings, that captures mechanical vibrations and converts them to an electrical signal that can be amplified and recorded (*see* pages 23–24, 26 & 42).

PLECTRUM or **PICK** A small flat plastic tool, usually triangular, that is used to pick or strum the strings (*see* pages 15 & 32–33).

POWER CHORD A chord composed of the root, a perfect fifth interval, and the root note doubled an octave higher. Often played through an overdriven amp in order to sound more powerful (*see* pages 21–22 & 46–47).

PULL-OFF A technique involving 'pulling' a finger off a string but leaving another finger still on the string lower down after that string has just been played in order to achieve a smooth sound (*see* pages 38–39).

RIFF A short rhythmic musical phrase, played repeatedly, which forms the 'hook' of a song (*see* pages 14–15 & 34–36).

STRING BENDING A technique involving pressing a string against the fretboard, striking a tone and then pushing the string up or down to make the pitch higher (*see* pages 17, 33 & 40).

SWEEP PICKING A technique that involves using a sweeping motion of the pick hand and matching the motion in the fretting hand in order to achieve a fast and fluid series of notes (*see* page 48).

TAPPING A technique using the fingers of one hand to 'tap' the strings against the fingerboard, sounding legato notes with the help of pull-offs or hammer-ons from the fretting hand (*see* page 48).

TREMOLO ARM or **WHAMMY BAR** A lever attached to the bridge and/or tailpiece that is used to alter the pitch of the strings to create a vibrato or pitch bend effect (*see* page 24).

TRILL A rapid series of hammer-ons and pull-offs between a single pair of notes (*see* page 39).

VIBRATO A kind of string bending in which the string is moved from side to side to add expression and vocal-like qualities (*see* pages 17 & 40).

Introduction

What is rock ... and why would you want to play it? Well, the term 'rock'n'roll', first applied to Elvis Presley's breakthrough music of the Fifties, came from black slang for what males and females get up to. So it's official: rock has always been sexy.

But when Elvis entered the US Army, everything quietened down and became pop music. It wasn't until the mid-Sixties, when Sgt Pepper taught the band to play, the Rolling Stones and Cream supercharged the blues and guitar heroes like Eric Clapton, Jeff Beck, Jimmy Page and Peter Green could be found around every corner, that rock split from pop to chart its own course.

It soon became obvious that the guitar players were the ones that got the girls. And that is the way it has always been. The singers may hog the limelight, but the six-stringers by their side are the

Jeff Beck, one of Britain's finest rock guitarists.

power behind the throne. And power, they say, is the ultimate aphrodisiac.

Guitar heroes have come in every shape and size, from the wild-eyed Jimi Hendrix to the top-hatted Slash, the Clash's Mick Jones to Arctic Monkey Jamie Cook. And there are many thousands more.

Legendary rock guitarist Jimi Hendrix performing live.

They have all put in the time to master their instrument, whether they admit it or not. And the likelihood is they still do. The objective is for man and guitar to be as one, the wood and metal a channel through which he expresses his innermost feelings. As one well-known player said: 'My guitar is not a thing.

It is an extension of myself. It is who I am.' So who was that guy? That was no guy, that was Joan Jett!

Yes, girls as well as boys can enjoy the satisfaction of communicating to their audience via the products of Fender, Gibson, Gretsch and Rickenbacker. Take a bow Heart's Nancy Wilson, Jennifer Batten, Lita Ford and the late great Kelly Johnson of Girlschool – let's hope there are more in the pipeline.

The best way to learn rock guitar, though, is not just from a book like this but by taking what you learn and playing with others. So once you have picked up the basics, get out of your bedroom and into a rehearsal studio, hall or scout hut with anyone who will play with you. That is when things begin to get interesting. It is the interaction with other musicians that makes the best music – and once you have got that, the sky is the limit.

We'll catch you on tour!

The Essentials

The Rhythm

The rhythm section of the band is usually thought to mean bass player and drummer. But the majority of rock bands, unless they fit the Who/Led Zeppelin three-piece template, have another element – a keyboard player or a rhythm guitarist. Once upon a time that would have been the less able six-stringer of the band – but since the likes of the Stones' Keith Richards and AC/DC's Malcolm Young have made churning out the riffs a profession to be proud of, the label of rhythm player is one to be worn with pride.

It is often the rhythm guitar you first hear as a great rock record bludgeons you about the ears. 'Brown Sugar'? 'Highway To Hell'? Those crunching chords are unmistakable, and they form part of the bedrock of the song. You need to be aware of what the bass and drums are doing: they and you should be as solid as a three-legged stool for the singer and lead guitar to 'sit' on. Also be aware of the 'one', the first beat of each bar which all three elements should hit together.

Rhythm guitarists are every bit as important as lead guitarists – don't let anyone tell you otherwise!

Renowned rhythm guitarist, the Stones' Keith Richards.

The Riffs

A riff is the major building block on which a rock song is built. It is a short phrase, played rhythmically, that is repeated so often that it forms the 'hook' to a song, like Deep Purple's 'Smoke On

Versatile guitarist and in-demand session player Jimmy Page.

14

The Water'. It is often confused with a lick, which may crop up only once or twice in a song, but is a recognizable component of a solo or lead part. So a lick can be a riff, but a riff is something more....

It can also be defined as the background for improvisation, so a riff is likely to be consistent and predictable rather than something that will vary. Imagine if Eric Clapton changed the signature riff to 'Layla' or Jimmy Page messed around with 'Whole Lotta Love' – it just would not happen. The audience expects to hear these riffs as recorded, but they are no less exciting for that. Leave the flash bits for the solo, these riffs need to be cranked out meatily and at maximum volume.

Most guitarists use a plectrum to play riffs on the lower strings, using down strokes to maximize attack. But rules are made to be broken ... so pick up your axe and riff away!

The Lead

The lead guitarist is intended to be the band's instrumental 'voice', and the emotion he puts into his playing will be relied upon to take a song to another level. Some bands employ twin lead players, notably the Allman Brothers Band, Thin Lizzy and Iron Maiden. These will see one of the players 'falling back' into the rhythm role before coming forward to play solo or harmony lead. In bands like the Rolling Stones, Keith Richards admits it is hard to tell the difference. 'We cross over, there's no lead and rhythm. It's basically when you can't tell who's doing what. It's simple but it's tight. That's what rock'n'roll has to be.'

Lead playing requires knowledge of scales, which many people see as patterns on the fretboard. Most solos will start on the root note of the chord and progress up or down the scale. Once that has been

Irish hard rockers Thin Lizzy, noted for their twin lead guitars.

achieved, the icing on the cake can be applied in the shape of vibrato, string bending, double-stops and other techniques. Although, it is important to remember that too many notes can detract from the overall effect. Play with feeling, not as fast as your fingers will let you, and you will impress every listener.

Chords & Scales

Guitar solos are played over a sequence of chords or riffs that will dictate what the lead guitarist plays. There are notes that will feel 'right' and notes that won't.

The pentatonic musical scale with five pitches per octave is the basis for most rock solos. The major guitar scale corresponds to the Ionian mode in the modal system and is the 'happy-sounding' scale, while the minor guitar scale, the basic 'sad-sounding' scale, corresponds with the Aeolian mode. The choice of whether to use major pentatonic or minor pentatonic can be by ear. If one doesn't sound right, the other one should work perfectly.

Normally a minor scale can only be played in a minor key and a major in a major key, but playing a pentatonic minor solo over a major chord

Major pentatonic scale

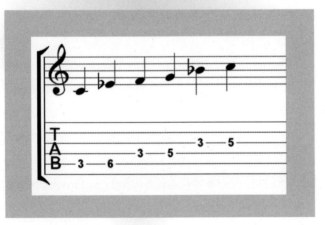

Minor pentatonic scale

progression results in flattened or 'blue' notes. There is also a variation known as the blues scale where a flattened fifth is added between the fourth and fifth. The blues scale in A adds an E flat to the usual A-C-D-E-G, adding colour to the progression: this is known as a chromatic note.

Scales are based on patterns on the fretboard, and can be transposed by moving that pattern up or down the fretboard. So once you have mastered the technique, you just need to identify what key the song is in and take it from there.

Chords under the solos may be played with open strings – most usually at the bottom end of the neck – or as barre chords, which can be transposed up the neck. If playing the barre chord of F, for instance, advancing it one fret towards the bridge will give you the chord of F sharp, two frets will turn it into G.

Power Chords

Some say power chords, which typically comprise two notes, are not chords at all but intervals; they maintain that a chord must have three notes as this defines whether it is a major or a minor. Be that as it may, power chords – composed of the root, a perfect fifth interval, and the root note doubled an octave above – are important building blocks in the making of a rock song.

The easiest way to play a power chord is on the bottom three (E, A, D) strings. This is simpler than, say, starting with the root note on the A string as the three strings you have to avoid playing (G, B, E) are all together on the other side of the neck. If your root note is on the A string and you are playing the A, D and G strings, then you must avoid or mute the bottom E.

Conversely, power chords using the top three (G, B, E) strings are also relatively simple as the strings are grouped together on one side of the fretboard. The effect of playing the three thinnest strings will be less powerful, but will cut through more if that is your intention.

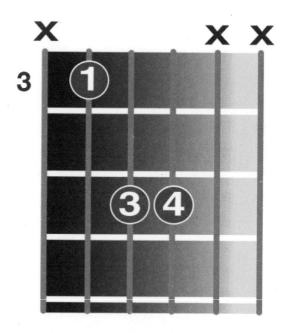

C5 power chord

Getting Ready to Play

Instruments & Equipment

Get any well-known guitarist to pick up half a dozen instruments in turn, and his style should be recognizable whatever he plays, from a beginners' guitar to a top of the range Gibson. The same goes for amplifiers, from the smallest 15-watt combo to a Marshall amp through a four 12-inch speaker cabinet. But there will be major differences in the sound that emerges. This is due to several factors.

Guitar pickups come in two varieties, single coil and humbucker, and each has a different, distinctive sound. The single-coil pickup is used by the Fender Stratocaster, which has three. This has a relatively thin, trebly output that cuts through the backing. But it also has 'in between' positions that allow the middle and bridge or middle and neck pickups to be used simultaneously, but out of phase, for a unique funky sound.

Gibson-type guitars invariably feature humbuckers whose thicker tone is quite different to a single-coil pickup. In fact it is two single coils wired together to reduce noise. Many modern guitars feature both single coil and humbucking pickups to give the player a wider variety of sounds.

Another way of making your sound distinctive is the tremolo arm or 'whammy bar', an optional extra on many guitar makes. This lets you alter the pitch of the strings by changing string tension up or down, pulling or pushing as you play.

No matter how much you pay for your electric guitar, it will only sound as good as the amp it is played through. You have a choice between valve and 'tube'-based amplification or transistorized amplification. Transistor amps are cheaper and more reliable, but lack the warmth of their valve

The perfect combo – a Fender Strat and a Vox amp.

counterparts. We now have the best of both worlds, however, in the shape of 'modelling' amps, which can approximate the sound of classic valve amps.

One of those 'tube' classics is the Vox AC30. This is a combination (combo), which includes both amplifier and speakers and is often adequate for small venues. Most guitarists start off with a combo. However, when rock bands moved from clubs to theatres and stadia, bands like Cream and the Who kicked out the combo and combined a powerful separate amplifier with a 4x12 (four 12-inch) speaker cabinet. This was clearly not as easy to transport but made certain they could be heard.

Amplifiers used to come with just treble, bass and volume controls; now there can be a mystifying array of knobs and faders. Most have at least 3-band EQ (equalization, i.e. bass, mid, and treble tone controls) with two channels that can be plugged into. Some guitarists use a footswitch to change between them mid-song, setting up a 'clean' and a 'dirty' (overdrive) sound to be used during verses and solos respectively.

A footswitch allows you to change guitar sounds during performances.

Tuning

Tuning is vital. If instruments are not in tune both with themselves and each other, the effect will not be a pleasant one. Fortunately digital tuners are now standard, and should be an essential part of your pedal board. Temperature and humidity can affect tuning, as can the power with which you hit the strings, how old they are and the effectiveness of your machine heads (tuning keys), so don't assume all will be well after you leave the dressing room.

The standard guitar tuning of E-A-D-G-B-E is far from the only choice. Slide guitarists use 'open tuning', in which a chord is played by the open strings. The use of a slide transposes this to any position along the fretboard.

The term 'modified tuning' is used to denote the practice of dropping a string or strings, which is common in modern rock. The easiest, Drop D, lowers (drops) the sixth (heaviest) string from an E down to a D. This makes it easier to play power chords on the lowest three strings. Some bands down-tune every string by a semitone or more to get a heavier sound. In this case, the chord shapes stay the same but everything will be half a tone flatter than played.

Using an electronic tuner is the simplest way to tune an instrument.

Warming Up

Music may come from the head and heart, but your body gives the physical delivery – and that is why guitarists should, like boy scouts, be prepared. Just as with athletes and footballers, the best results will come when you have woken up the relevant muscles, rather than starting from cold.

Stretching your wrists, hands and fingers is a good starting point, and should precede any actual playing. Pressing palm to palm and bending each hand in turn to make a 90-degree angle – a little beyond, if possible – can be followed by bending

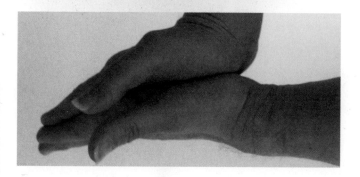

back individual fingers. Repeat the process three or four times, then try pairs of fingers.

Having warmed up your hands and fingers, exercises with the guitar can include scales or arpeggios. Start slow, then speed up, changing your picking patterns and gradually incorporating hammer-ons and pull-offs.

Exercise can also help you avoid tendonitis, carpal tunnel syndrome and other repetitive stress injuries.

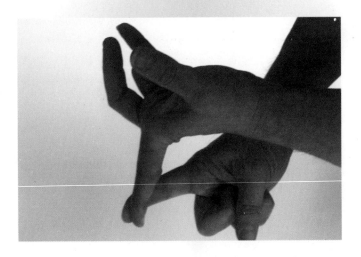

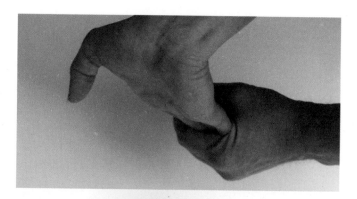

But they can also help you play better and achieve greater speed. Athletes and footballers may not have a lot to do with rock'n'roll, but taking a leaf out of their book has worked for guitarists. So take care of yourself – no one else will!

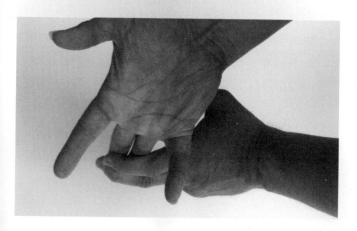

Techniques

How to Use
Plectrums & Strings

Nine out of 10 guitarists use a plastic plectrum to hit the strings, rather than fingers alone, but it is also possible to combine the two. The usual position is between the thumb and index finger, the thumb covering the plectrum at the first joint on the finger.

Plectrums range in thickness from around 0.44 mm to 1 mm and beyond, and are classed as light, medium or heavy. The thicker the plectrum the louder riffs and single-string solos will ring out, though light-gauge ones are often preferable for strumming chords.

The picking hand controls timing and volume of the notes, and may also be used to damp the strings. The movement of the plectrum should be mainly controlled by the wrist, with minimum movement of the right arm itself. Tensing the arm and moving from the elbow will restrict the ability to build up speed and smoothness and should be avoided. Practise up strokes and down strokes, first on one string and then on different strings, and your fluency will soon increase.

The gauge of the strings you play will affect your sound. Thick strings (.014–.059) are more suited to rock riffs but are harder to play, while lighter strings (.010–.047) allow easier bending of single notes.

Playing Riffs

It may be stating the obvious, but playing guitar riffs is a game of two hands. You will have to pay attention not only to what your left hand is doing on the fretboard (assuming you are right handed), but also what the right hand is doing to pick the strings. Both must be perfect in their own right before they are integrated to produce the effect you want.

This may sound daunting, but the upside is that you can master riffs much quicker than whole songs. Be aware of what chords you are passing through as it will help you make more sense of the patterns; seemingly complex riffs are often based on simple harmonic structures. Simplicity is the key to a memorable riff – be it one, two or even four bars in length. And they need to be played efficiently, with no unnecessary widdling. Make sure each note rings clearly, without any hint of fret buzz.

If, say, you are choosing to play the distinctive riff of Aerosmith's 'Walk This Way' you won't be able to approach the speed on the record straight away. Joe Perry had years of practice! It might help to find clips of the song being played on YouTube to give you hints as to where on the neck he plays it, picking patterns, etc. – or try any number of internet sites for tablature. But work up to the speed you hear, don't play along to the recording and establish bad habits.

If you want to get better, just play at every opportunity.

Riffs will tend to be chunky and attacking, and played on the guitar's lower strings, so to do them justice there are several factors to consider. A heavier gauge of string, humbucking pickups and a weightier guitar with more sustain will help you towards the sound you seek, while a valve amplifier, or one with the ability to emulate one, may also add body to the figures you are playing. Playing down strokes only will add power, but again see how the original guitarist does it and experiment.

Incorporating open strings into riffs is a difficult skill, but worthwhile mastering to add variety to your playing. Keith Richards is a past master of this, and he often uses open tunings to help him – or takes the bottom E string off completely. But bear in mind retuning your guitar on stage is impractical unless you have a spare you can leave in a different tuning.

Playing Lead Solos

Some rock fans love guitar solos, others (rather fewer, we suspect) loathe them. Similarly, for guitarists they can be a challenge or a chore. If you want to keep your soloing fresh rather than play the same thing every night, you need to leave room for improvisation – to go where the mood takes you. So it is a good idea to give your solo a structure: a beginning, middle and end.

While multiple strings are used for chords, solos will usually involve playing single strings one at a time. To avoid sounding thin and tinny you may need a booster pedal to push your volume and possibly add an element of distortion. It is also worthwhile doing your homework as to keys and scales: using a minor pentatonic scale against a major chord sequence, for instance, can impart a very bluesy flavour to a solo.

Solo techniques 1: pull-off with two fingers

Solo techniques 2: hammer-on with three fingers

Solo techniques 3: string bends – two-string and single-string versions

There are techniques you can use to add character to your soloing. Trills, hammer-ons and pull-offs are methods of playing more than one note with a single pick of the string, rather like a saxophone player playing multiple notes with a single breath.

Hammering on is achieved by placing another finger forcefully onto the same string at a higher fret than the one first played. Pull-offs are the opposite, the left-hand finger being removed with a plucking motion to obtain the desired volume and effect. Trills combine the two techniques to achieve a rippling sound. Sliding strings and double-stops are also effective.

A unison note bend involves playing two notes together (in unison), with one fretted normally and the other being bent up to the required pitch: this was a favoured technique of Jimi Hendrix and, later, Carlos Santana. It is most effective on the first and second, or second and third strings, and is most e a s i l y accomplished with first (fretting) and third (bending) fingers and, when it works,

Solo techniques 4: vibrato

has an almost human sound. Once you have accomplished bending up, try picking a bent string and letting it return to its usual position.

Vibrato is another kind of string bending, but a more subtle form in which the string is moved from side to side rather than up and down. Free's Paul Kossoff and blues legend B.B. King are among those who made this technique a trademark.

Rhythm Guitar & Chops

As a rhythm guitarist, you are locking into and augmenting the rhythm provided by bass and drums, acting as the link between that and the lead guitar and vocal. Much of rock rhythm playing will be 'straight eight', in other words eight $1/8$ notes or quavers to each bar. This gives the driving feel many rock songs need. Then there is the 'clave' or Bo Diddley-style syncopated beat, which involves leaving space in your playing: try saying 'shave and a haircut – two bits' and you'll get the picture.

Again, while the straight eight will generally be played with down strokes only on the guitar's lowest strings, variations may require a combination of up and down strokes.

You may also be playing basic riffs and using palm muting to add dynamics to your parts. Palm muting the strings at the bridge lets you have instant control of your volume, while playing semi-muted strings can add a threatening edge.

Many players spend more of their time playing as a rhythm guitarist than a lead guitarist – one example being the Who's Pete Townshend . This was partly due to his penchant for ringing, open chords but also because bass player John Entwistle supplied many of the lead lines on his four string. Of course unlike a two-guitar band where the rhythm guitarist's job is defined, a lone guitarist must cover all the bases.

Rhythm guitarists often choose equipment that 'fattens' their sound, for example humbucking pickups and valve (or valve emulating) amplification. Strings will usually be a heavier gauge than the lead guitar.

Playing in a funkier style than straight rock is a challenge for any rhythm guitarist, as you may find yourself locking in with the snare drum on beats two and four while the bass does its own thing. The soul/R&B classic 'Midnight Hour', for instance, saw rhythm guitarist Steve Cropper playing a down stroke on beats two and four of every bar, damping the chords after they were struck.

Such musical projects may require the rhythm guitarist to come up with different ways of playing each chord. That way you can change the sound of a chord while you are playing it: one master of this was Nile Rodgers of Chic, who could give a feeling of movement even though he was riffing on the same chord. It is a good weapon to have in your locker.

Good rhythm guitar requires more than a bit of strumming!

Playing Open & Barre Chords

Open chords, most often played on the lower frets, are the first ones guitarists learn. They have the advantage of containing open strings, so will be loud, but these chords often need to be muted as they will ring out as long as the guitar sustain will allow. Similarly, chords that are played up the neck with open strings may be uneven, so care must be taken to fret them strongly so that all strings sound.

Barre chords are the opposite to open chords, as all strings played are fretted. They offer a method of playing chords up and down the fretboard using basic shapes but using the index finger as if it were the nut at the peghead end. Moving the E shape up a fret turns it into F. The concept is relatively simple but can be difficult for the beginner to master as it

E major chord with open strings

involves using all fingers of the fretting hand and exerting sufficient pressure with your index finger so that all the strings ring out clearly. The position of the thumb directly behind the index finger at the back of the neck is crucial. Barre chords are easier to play higher up the neck from A major upwards. If you still have problems, use the side of your first finger and bring your elbow into your body a little more.

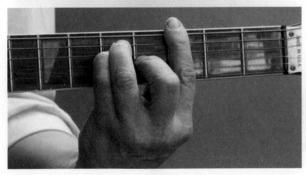

G major barre chord

Playing Power Chords

Power chords, made up of the root and fifth notes of a chord, are the building blocks of many heavy rock classics. An example of a power chord is A, whose root note is A and fifth is E; the addition of A an octave above completes the chord. In this case the notes would probably be played on the bottom three strings.

E major power chord with E and B octaves driving a really big sound.

While major chords have a major third and minor chords have a minor third, power chords are different. They lack a third completely, and this makes them sound powerful and distinctive, especially when played through an overdriven amp.

Jimi Hendrix was very partial to this 'ambiguous' chord while Pete Townshend also used them, often on the bottom three strings but also sometimes with an open string added to give a trademark 'jangle'. The 'windmill' right arm technique is optional but always a crowd pleaser!

The impact of a power chord (also known as a five chord) can be demonstrated by playing one in comparison with its major equivalent, dialling in a fair helping of overdrive. The power chord wins every time! It is a trick bands from Black Sabbath to Metallica have used on their greatest songs and one well worth adding to your armoury.

Picking & Muting

Picking can be up, down or, more usually, alternate, using downward and upward strokes of the plectrum. Sweep picking involves matching a 'sweeping' motion of the pick in the right hand to produce a fast and fluid series of notes, while tapping means using the fingers of one hand to 'tap' the strings against the fingerboard, sounding legato notes with the help of pull-offs or hammer-ons from the left (fretting) hand.

Palm muting is a technique you may well have started using before you knew what it was. It is

Tapping techniques require very fast finger skills.

carried out using the side of the right hand, despite the name, and stops the strings vibrating to a greater or lesser degree depending on how much pressure is applied. The result of plucking a string that is simultaneously being muted is quite evocative.

Practice will show how much pressure you need to apply with the side or heel of your picking hand to achieve the desired effect. The nearer you place your muting hand to the guitar bridge the more effective it will be. Using distortion with the technique is very effective, as is wah-wah, while picking up and down will give a driving feel to your playing. The tablature indication of palm muting is the initials PM.

Palm muting is an essential part of every guitarists' armoury.

Using the Right Effects

When effects were first devised to add colour and variety to music they were strictly confined to the studio. Then the effects pedal appeared in the early Sixties, made possible by transistor technology. The wah-wah was used by Jimi Hendrix and Eric Clapton, as they found it could add an almost human emotion to their playing with its ability to change the guitar's tone with a movement of the foot.

Reverb, often used in the studio to add depth, was another popular effect, while fuzz boxes, the popular name for early distortion pedals, beefed up many a solo. They did this by clipping the signal's waveform, and distortion remains the most popular guitar effect today.

Overdrive pedals offer the classic rock sound.

Delay was obtainable via a Copicat or Echoplex, which employed tape loops – these days digital technology is much neater and practical, though vintage effects pedals attract high prices on the collectors' market. Some users employ a single echo for a 'slap' effect, but players like John Martyn and U2's the Edge have fully embraced delay as part of their signature sound.

Phasing and flanging were both studio effects that guitarists craved once introduced in the Sixties, and both are now very much a part of their arsenal. The familiar 'whooshing noise' of phasing was popular in the Seventies with groups like the Doobie Brothers.

The wah-wah can be used for expressive tonal effects

Chorus pedals work by
mixing a delayed signal
with the original sound.

Compression evens out the volume of the guitar's output – a boon for those whose picking skills are less than perfect. It also gives the sound a distinctive Eighties flavour. By contrast, chorus thickens the sound by splitting the guitar signal in two, modulating the second signal's pitch and mixing it back in with the original 'dry' signal. This gives the effect of several guitarists playing the same thing at the same time.

With many guitarists 'daisy-chaining' a large number of pedals on stage, it has become mandatory to have a noise gate that will ensure the hiss and background noise is not heard between songs. Until the guitar signal exceeds a threshold figure, the gate will remain closed.

The trend in the twenty-first century has been to combine the pedals in a neat multi-effects unit. Purists will say something has been sacrificed with this clever use of digital technology, but for most purposes and performers the approximate sounds the units deliver are more than adequate. Famous names include Zoom and Line 6.

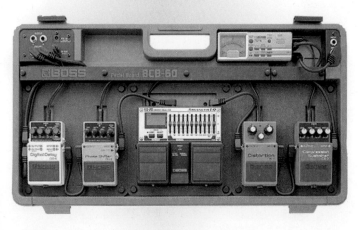

Pedal boards can be used to control a large rack of devices.

The Music
Using the Examples

The examples are divided by type of music and organized chronolgically for ease of use. Each type of music is indicated by a tab at the edge of every page and each is given a series of generic examples for rhythm, riffs and lead play. Both notation and tab is provided, although chord boxes are given where appropriate.

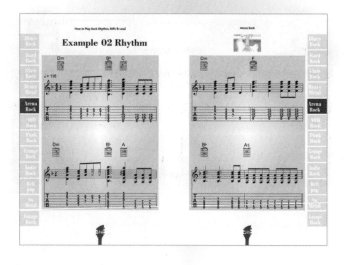

The Music

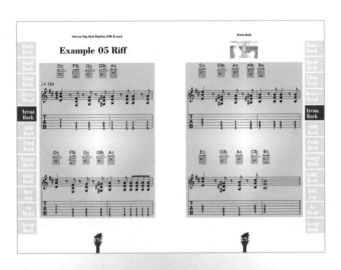

Blues
Rock

Hard
Rock

Glam
Rock

Heavy
Metal

Arena
Rock

AOR
Rock

Punk
Rock

Grunge
Rock

Indie
Rock

Brit
pop

Nu
Metal

Garage
Rock

Blues Rock

The blues boom of the Sixties was built on the 12-bar musical formula. The Rolling Stones were typical of bands like the Animals and the Pretty Things in graduating from covers of blues originals to self-penned classics. With volume came feedback and distortion thanks to the Who, who attempted to bring their stage act into the recording studio. John Mayall's Bluesbreakers With Eric Clapton (1966) became a primer for a generation of rock guitarists to come as Clapton sent studio meters into the red with a Gibson Les Paul and a 50-watt amplifier. Meanwhile Jeff Beck, Clapton's replacement in the Yardbirds, clawed otherworldly sounds from his Fender, following up his stint with two solo albums of supercharged blues.

Slide guitar was adopted by musicians such as Duane Allman of the Allman Brothers Band whose soaring slide part was the climax of 'Layla', and Jeremy Spencer, the second guitarist of Fleetwood Mac. Mac's other guitarist, Peter Green, pushed the boundaries of blues rock to include psychedelia.

Blues Rock

Hard Rock

Glam Rock

Heavy Metal

Arena Rock

AOR Rock

Punk Rock

Grunge Rock

Indie Rock

Brit pop

Nu Metal

Garage Rock

Blues
Rock

Hard
Rock

Glam
Rock

Heavy
Metal

Arena
Rock

AOR
Rock

Punk
Rock

Grunge
Rock

Indie
Rock

Brit
pop

Nu
Metal

Garage
Rock

Example 01 Rhythm

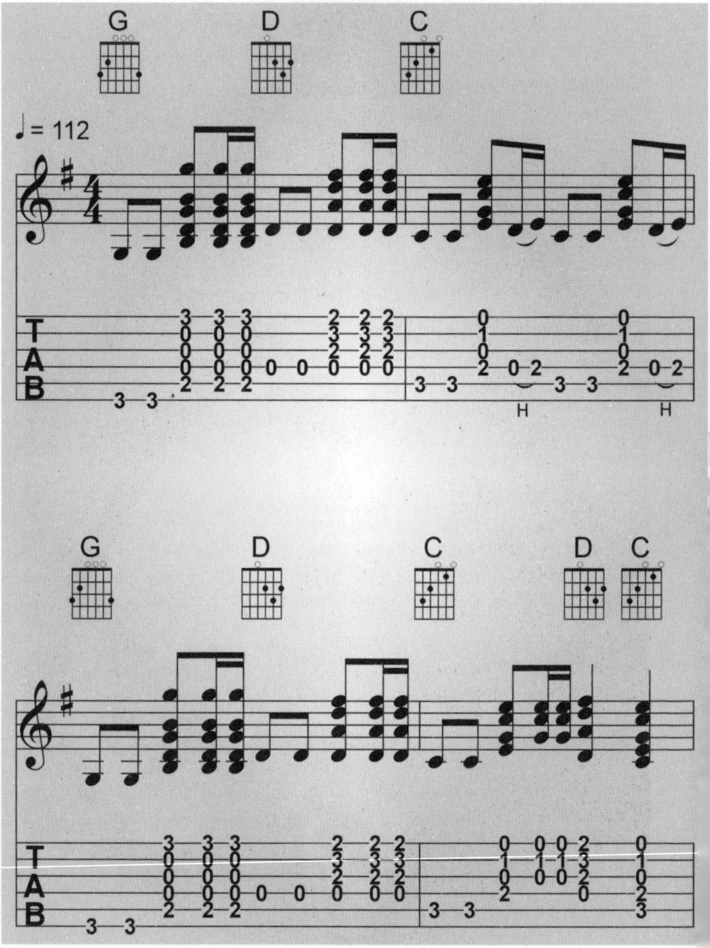

Blues Rock

Blues Rock

Hard Rock

Glam Rock

Heavy Metal

Arena Rock

AOR Rock

Punk Rock

Grunge Rock

Indie Rock

Brit pop

Nu Metal

Garage Rock

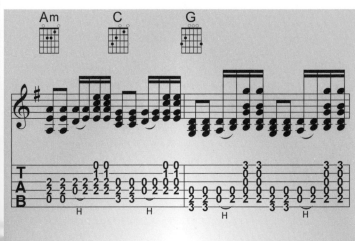

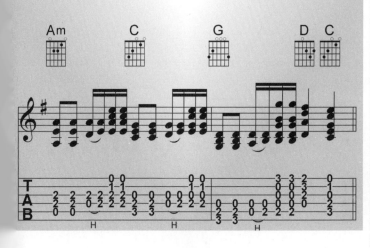

59

Example 02 Rhythm

Hard
Rock

Glam
Rock

Heavy
Metal

Arena
Rock

AOR
Rock

Punk
Rock

Grunge
Rock

Indie
Rock

Brit
pop

Nu
Metal

Garage
Rock

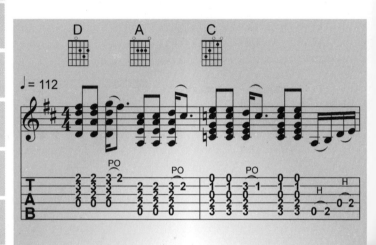

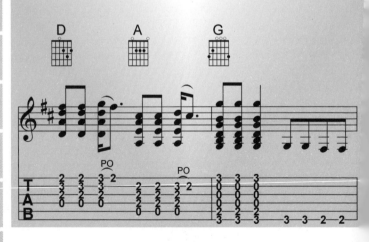

60

Blues Rock

Blues
Rock

Hard
Rock

Glam
Rock

Heavy
Metal

Arena
Rock

AOR
Rock

Punk
Rock

Grunge
Rock

Indie
Rock

Brit
pop

Nu
Metal

Garage
Rock

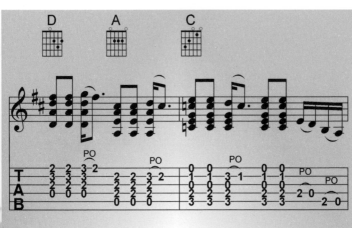

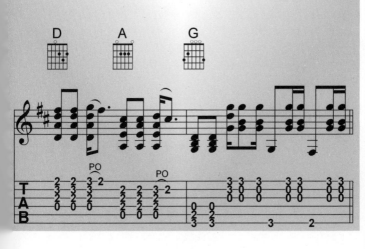

61

Blues
Rock

Hard
Rock

Glam
Rock

Heavy
Metal

Arena
Rock

AOR
Rock

Punk
Rock

Grunge
Rock

Indie
Rock

Brit
pop

Nu
Metal

Garage
Rock

Example 03 Rhythm

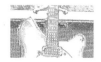

Blues
Rock

Hard
Rock

Glam
Rock

Heavy
Metal

Arena
Rock

AOR
Rock

Punk
Rock

Grunge
Rock

Indie
Rock

Brit
pop

Nu
Metal

Garage
Rock

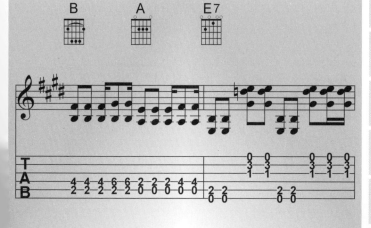

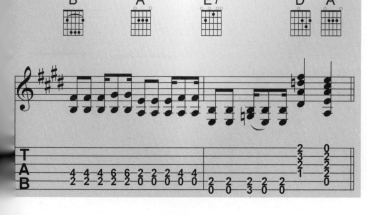

Example 04 Rhythm

Blues
Rock

Hard
Rock

Glam
Rock

Heavy
Metal

Arena
Rock

AOR
Rock

Punk
Rock

Grunge
Rock

Indie
Rock

Brit
pop

Nu
Metal

Garage
Rock

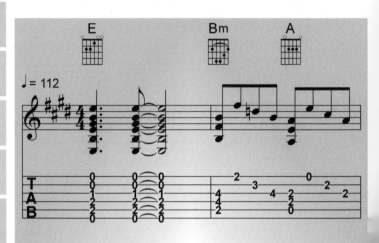

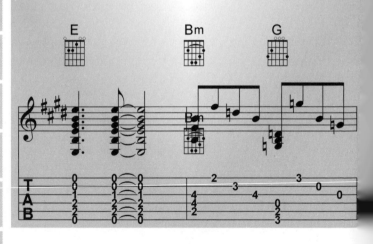

Blues Rock

Blues Rock

Hard Rock

Glam Rock

Heavy Metal

Arena Rock

AOR Rock

Punk Rock

Grunge Rock

Indie Rock

Brit pop

Nu Metal

Garage Rock

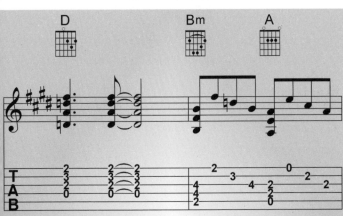

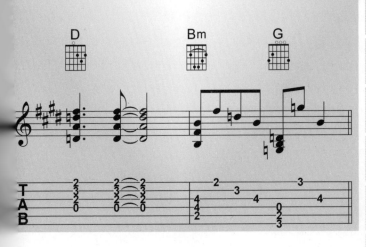

Example 05 Riff

Blues Rock

Hard Rock

Glam Rock

Heavy Metal

Arena Rock

AOR Rock

Punk Rock

Grunge Rock

Indie Rock

Brit pop

Nu Metal

Garage Rock

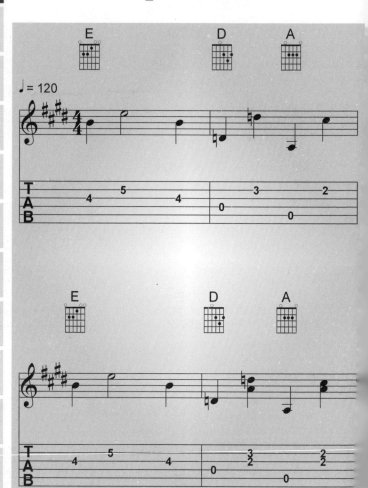

Blues Rock

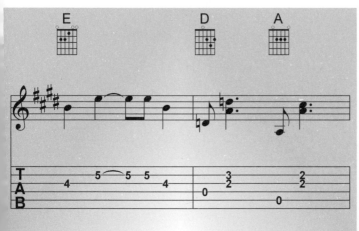

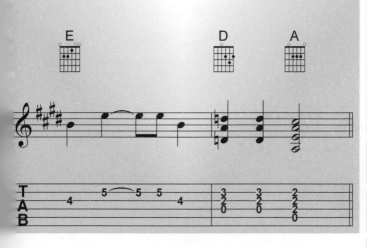

Blues
Rock

Hard
Rock

Glam
Rock

Heavy
Metal

Arena
Rock

AOR
Rock

Punk
Rock

Grunge
Rock

Indie
Rock

Brit
pop

Nu
Metal

Garage
Rock

Blues Rock

Hard Rock

Glam Rock

Heavy Metal

Arena Rock

AOR Rock

Punk Rock

Grunge Rock

Indie Rock

Brit pop

Nu Metal

Garage Rock

Example 06 Riff

Blues Rock

Blues Rock

Hard Rock

Glam Rock

Heavy Metal

Arena Rock

AOR Rock

Punk Rock

Grunge Rock

Indie Rock

Brit pop

Nu Metal

Garage Rock

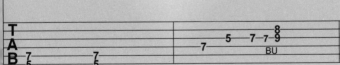

Example 07 Riff

Blues Rock

Hard Rock

Glam Rock

Heavy Metal

Arena Rock

AOR Rock

Punk Rock

Grunge Rock

Indie Rock

Brit pop

Nu Metal

Garage Rock

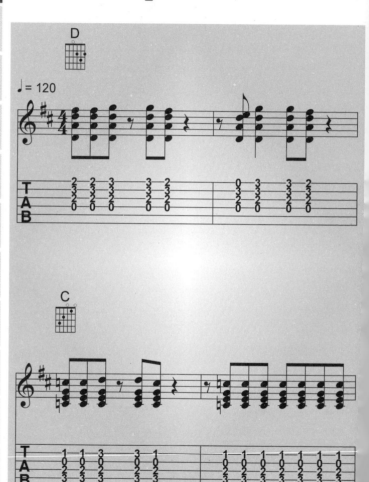

Blues Rock

Blues Rock

Hard Rock

Glam Rock

Heavy Metal

Arena Rock

AOR Rock

Punk Rock

Grunge Rock

Indie Rock

Brit pop

Nu Metal

Garage Rock

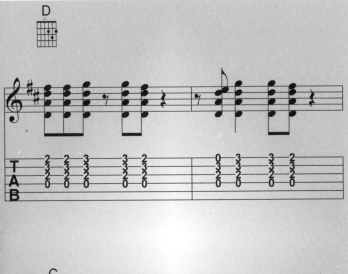

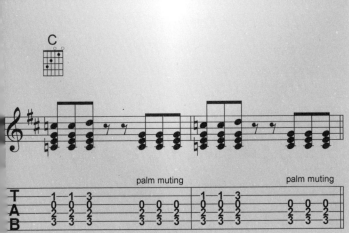

Example 08 Riff

Blues Rock

Blues Rock

Hard Rock

Glam Rock

Heavy Metal

Arena Rock

AOR Rock

Punk Rock

Grunge Rock

Indie Rock

Brit pop

Nu Metal

Garage Rock

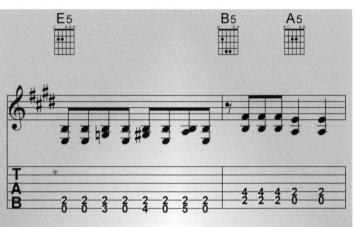

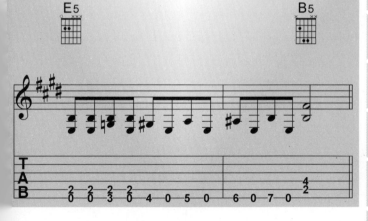

Example 09 Lead

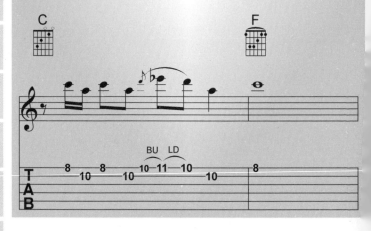

Blues Rock

Hard Rock

Glam Rock

Heavy Metal

Arena Rock

AOR Rock

Punk Rock

Grunge Rock

Indie Rock

Brit pop

Nu Metal

Garage Rock

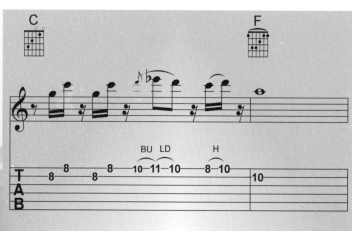

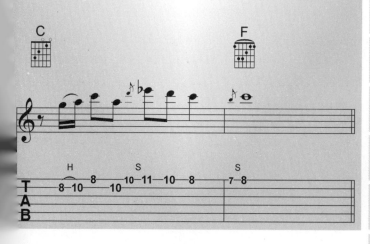

Example 10 Lead

Hard
Rock

Glam
Rock

Heavy
Metal

Arena
Rock

AOR
Rock

Punk
Rock

Grunge
Rock

Indie
Rock

Brit
pop

Nu
Metal

Garage
Rock

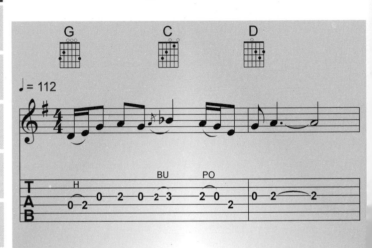

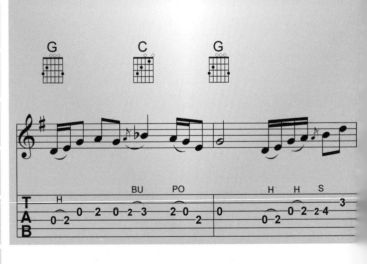

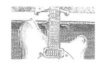

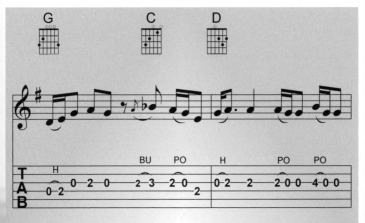

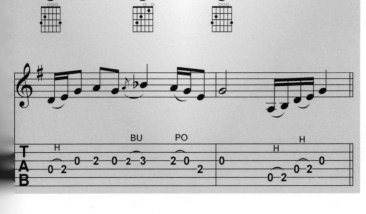

Blues
Rock

Hard
Rock

Glam
Rock

Heavy
Metal

Arena
Rock

AOR
Rock

Punk
Rock

Grunge
Rock

Indie
Rock

Brit
pop

Nu
Metal

Garage
Rock

Example 11 Lead

Blues Rock

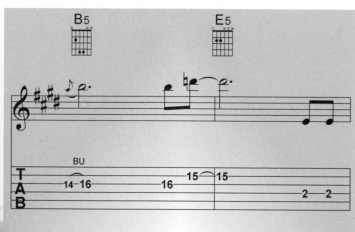

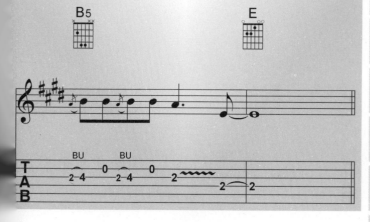

Blues
Rock

Hard
Rock

Glam
Rock

Heavy
Metal

Arena
Rock

AOR
Rock

Punk
Rock

Grunge
Rock

Indie
Rock

Brit
pop

Nu
Metal

Garage
Rock

Example 12 Lead

Blues
Rock

Hard
Rock

Glam
Rock

Heavy
Metal

Arena
Rock

AOR
Rock

Punk
Rock

Grunge
Rock

Indie
Rock

Brit
pop

Nu
Metal

Garage
Rock

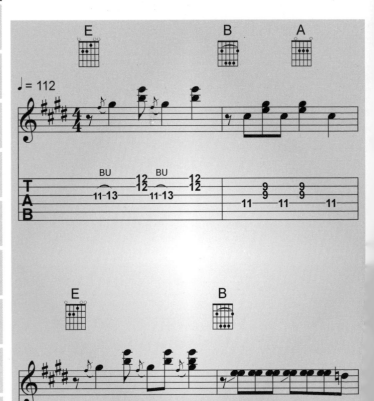

Blues Rock

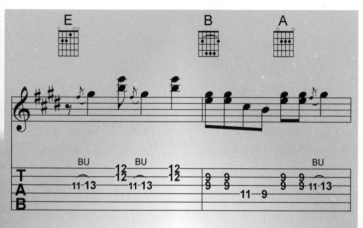

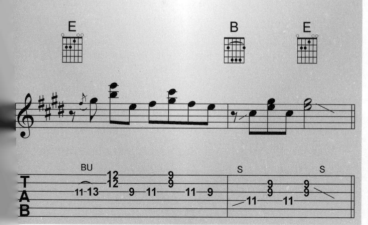

Blues
Rock

Hard
Rock

Glam
Rock

Heavy
Metal

Arena
Rock

AOR
Rock

Punk
Rock

Grunge
Rock

Indie
Rock

Brit
pop

Nu
Metal

Garage
Rock

Blues
Rock

Hard
Rock

Glam
Rock

Heavy
Metal

Arena
Rock

AOR
Rock

Punk
Rock

Grunge
Rock

Indie
Rock

Brit
pop

Nu
Metal

Garage
Rock

Hard Rock

Hard rock guitar developed from and shares some of the characteristics of blues rock. Dynamics were more highly developed, while the combination of Gibson guitar and Marshall amplifier as pioneered by Led Zeppelin's Jimmy Page became the benchmark. Sometimes guitars were down-tuned, as pioneered by Black Sabbath's Tony Iommi, to give a doomy effect – this has been much imitated in many styles since. But Eddie Van Halen's overnight arrival in the guitar players' hall of fame with his band's eponymous 1978 debut album shook up the established order. His tapping on the track 'Eruption' in particular was positively revolutionary.

Even second-division bands like UFO and Budgie provided guitar heroes in the shape of Michael Schenker and Tony Bourge, playing ever harsher, heavier riffs to an eager audience. Metallica would later cite Budgie as an influence, while Guns N'Roses said the same of Scotland's Nazareth, whose guitarist Manny Charlton would have been their producer had fate not intervened.

Blues Rock

Hard Rock

Glam Rock

Heavy Metal

Arena Rock

AOR Rock

Punk Rock

Grunge Rock

Indie Rock

Brit pop

Nu Metal

Garage Rock

Example 01 Rhythm

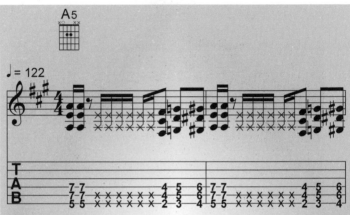

With distortion.
Drop all strings by 1 semitone.

Hard Rock

Blues Rock

Hard Rock

Glam Rock

Heavy Metal

Arena Rock

AOR Rock

Punk Rock

Grunge Rock

Indie Rock

Brit pop

Nu Metal

Garage Rock

E5

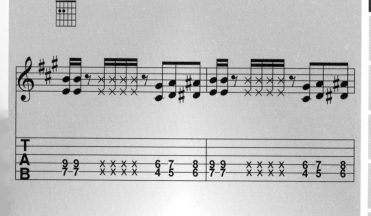

Example 02 Rhythm

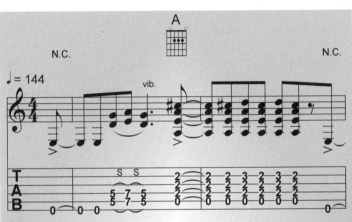

With distortion.
Drop all strings by 1 semitone.

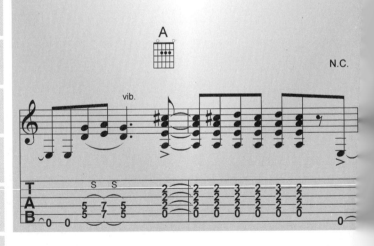

Hard Rock

Blues Rock

Hard Rock

Glam Rock

Heavy Metal

Arena Rock

AOR Rock

Punk Rock

Grunge Rock

Indie Rock

Brit pop

Nu Metal

Garage Rock

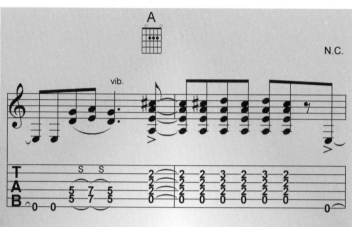

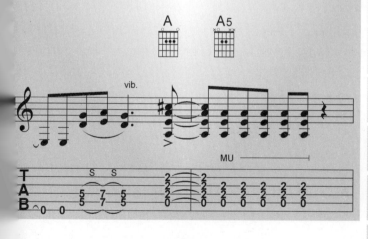

Example 03 Rhythm

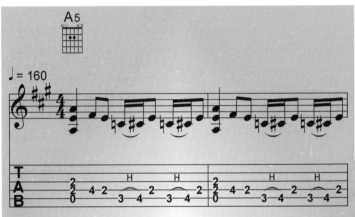

A5

♩ = 160

With distortion.

Hard Rock

Blues
Rock

**Hard
Rock**

Glam
Rock

Heavy
Metal

Arena
Rock

AOR
Rock

Punk
Rock

Grunge
Rock

Indie
Rock

Brit
pop

Nu
Metal

Garage
Rock

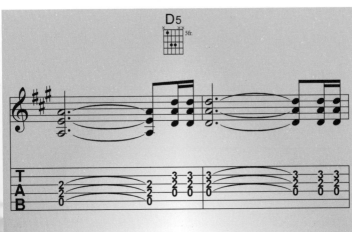

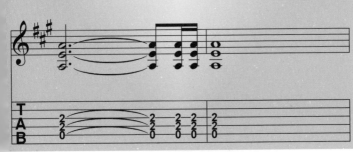

Example 04 Rhythm

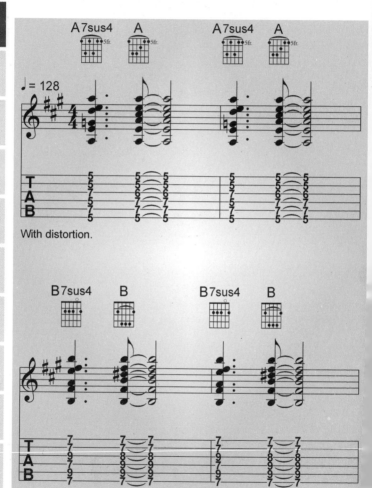

With distortion.

Hard Rock

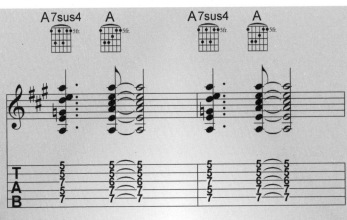

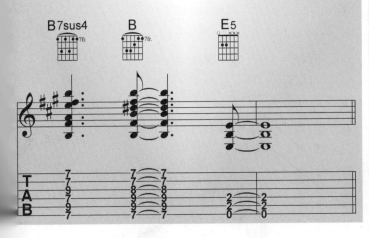

Blues Rock

Hard Rock

Glam Rock

Heavy Metal

Arena Rock

AOR Rock

Punk Rock

Grunge Rock

Indie Rock

Brit pop

Nu Metal

Garage Rock

Example 05 Riff

Blues Rock

Hard Rock

Glam Rock

Heavy Metal

Arena Rock

AOR Rock

Punk Rock

Grunge Rock

Indie Rock

Brit pop

Nu Metal

Garage Rock

With distortion.

Blues
Rock

**Hard
Rock**

Glam
Rock

Heavy
Metal

Arena
Rock

AOR
Rock

Punk
Rock

Grunge
Rock

Indie
Rock

Brit
pop

Nu
Metal

Garage
Rock

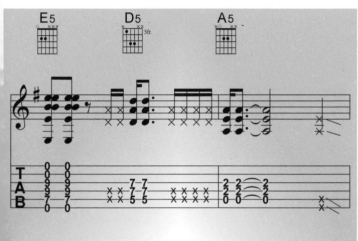

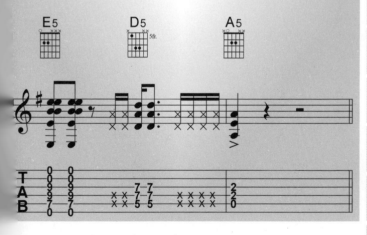

Example 06 Riff

With distortion.

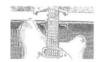

Blues Rock

Hard Rock

Glam Rock

Heavy Metal

Arena Rock

AOR Rock

Punk Rock

Grunge Rock

Indie Rock

Brit pop

Nu Metal

Garage Rock

Example 07 Riff

Blues
Rock

Hard
Rock

Glam
Rock

Heavy
Metal

Arena
Rock

AOR
Rock

Punk
Rock

Grunge
Rock

Indie
Rock

Brit
pop

Nu
Metal

Garage
Rock

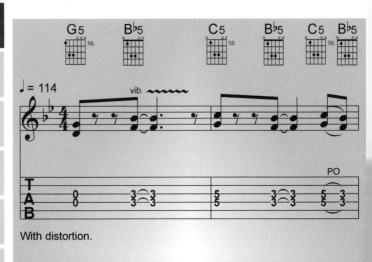

With distortion.

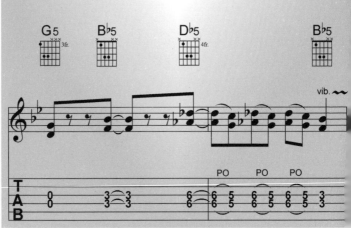

Hard Rock

Blues Rock

Hard Rock

Glam Rock

Heavy Metal

Arena Rock

AOR Rock

Punk Rock

Grunge Rock

Indie Rock

Brit pop

Nu Metal

Garage Rock

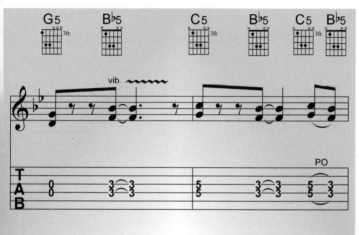

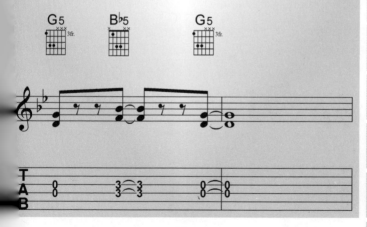

Example 08 Riff

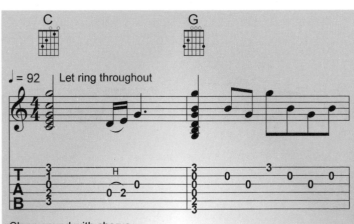

Clean sound with chorus.
Drop all strings by 1 semitone.

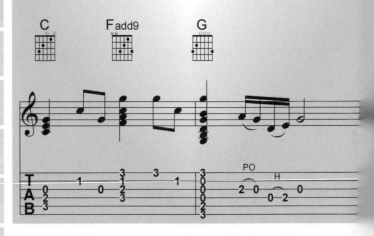

Hard Rock

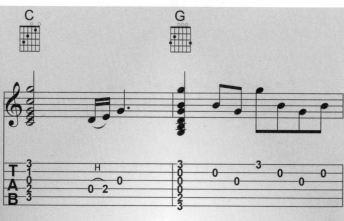

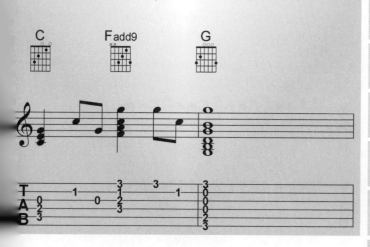

Blues Rock

Hard Rock

Glam Rock

Heavy Metal

Arena Rock

AOR Rock

Punk Rock

Grunge Rock

Indie Rock

Brit pop

Nu Metal

Garage Rock

Example 09 Lead

Blues Rock

Hard Rock

Glam Rock

Heavy Metal

Arena Rock

AOR Rock

Punk Rock

Grunge Rock

Indie Rock

Brit pop

Nu Metal

Garage Rock

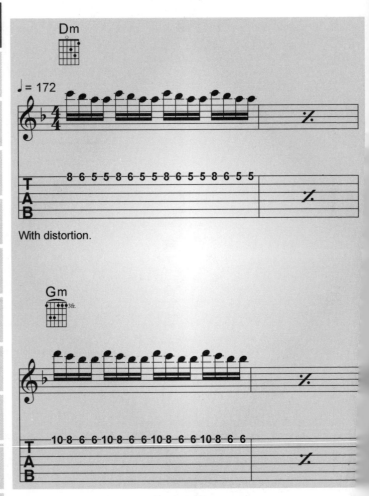

With distortion.

Hard Rock

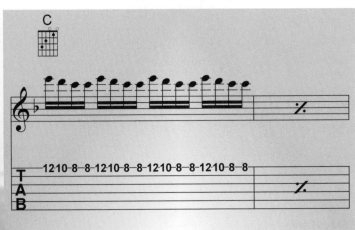

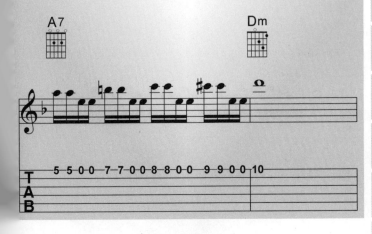

Blues Rock

Hard Rock

Glam Rock

Heavy Metal

Arena Rock

AOR Rock

Punk Rock

Grunge Rock

Indie Rock

Brit pop

Nu Metal

Garage Rock

Example 10 Lead

Blues
Rock

Hard
Rock

Glam
Rock

Heavy
Metal

Arena
Rock

AOR
Rock

Punk
Rock

Grunge
Rock

Indie
Rock

Brit
pop

Nu
Metal

Garage
Rock

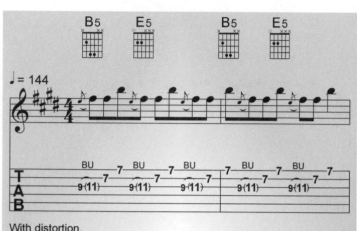

With distortion.
Drop all strings by 1 semitone.

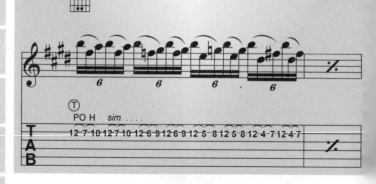

Blues
Rock

Hard
Rock

Glam
Rock

Heavy
Metal

Arena
Rock

AOR
Rock

Punk
Rock

Grunge
Rock

Indie
Rock

Brit
pop

Nu
Metal

Garage
Rock

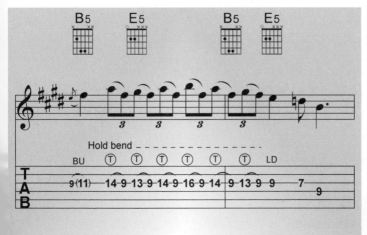

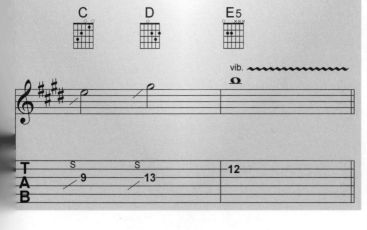

Example 11 Lead

Blues Rock

Hard Rock

Glam Rock

Heavy Metal

Arena Rock

AOR Rock

Punk Rock

Grunge Rock

Indie Rock

Brit pop

Nu Metal

Garage Rock

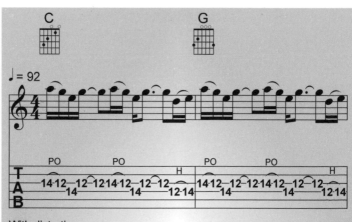

With distortion.

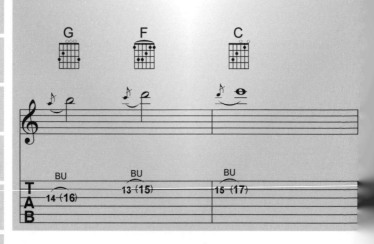

Hard Rock

Blues Rock

Hard Rock

Glam Rock

Heavy Metal

Arena Rock

AOR Rock

Punk Rock

Grunge Rock

Indie Rock

Brit pop

Nu Metal

Garage Rock

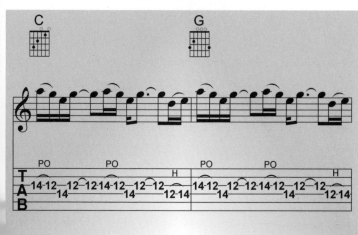

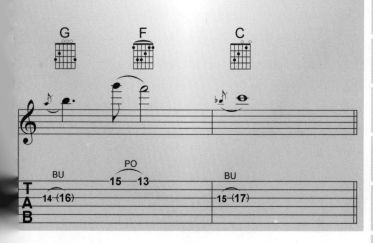

Example 12 Lead

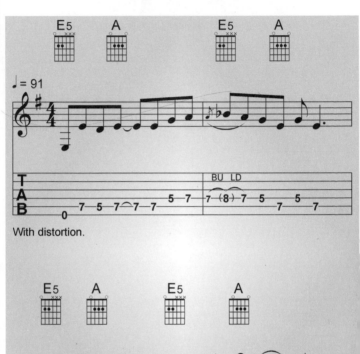

With distortion.

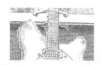

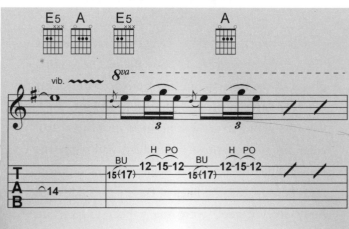

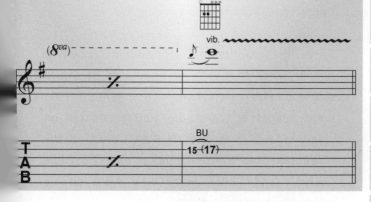

Blues Rock

Hard Rock

Glam Rock

Heavy Metal

Arena Rock

AOR Rock

Punk Rock

Grunge Rock

Indie Rock

Brit pop

Nu Metal

Garage Rock

Blues
Rock

Hard
Rock

Glam
Rock

Heavy
Metal

Arena
Rock

AOR
Rock

Punk
Rock

Grunge
Rock

Indie
Rock

Brit
pop

Nu
Metal

Garage
Rock

Glam Rock

The Glam Rock sound that swept the Seventies has often been revived since. Marc Bolan, the leading player of the time, graduated from acoustic guitar when Tyrannosaurus Rex plugged in and became T. Rex. The chord structures he used on his Les Paul were simple, repetitive but played with élan. His style rubbed off on David Bowie and his guitarist Mick Ronson, but the likes of Dave Hill (Slade) and Andy Scott (Sweet) were really heavy rockers in make-up. The riff of Sweet's 'Blockbuster' for instance was nicked from Muddy Waters' 'Manish Boy', while many of Slade's hooks were carried by Jimmy Lea's McCartney-esque bass.

Gary Glitter's Glitterband used simple, fuzz-ed up power chords that were then doubled by sax to sound at once powerful and retro – so many tricks were created in the studio and reproduced on stage. Indeed, as with Marc Bolan, much of the inspiration came from early rock'n'rollers like Eddie Cochran and Chuck Berry who were largely unfamiliar to teenage fans.

Blues
Rock

Hard
Rock

Glam
Rock

Heavy
Metal

Arena
Rock

AOR
Rock

Punk
Rock

Grunge
Rock

Indie
Rock

Brit
pop

Nu
Metal

Garage
Rock

Example 01 Rhythm

Glam Rock

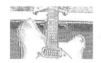

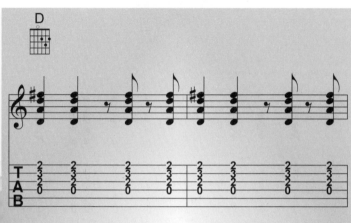

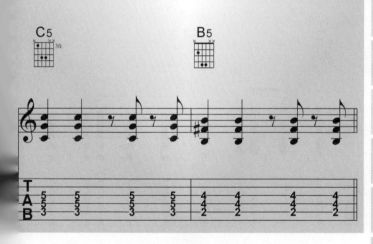

Blues
Rock

Hard
Rock

Glam
Rock

Heavy
Metal

Arena
Rock

AOR
Rock

Punk
Rock

Grunge
Rock

Indie
Rock

Brit
pop

Nu
Metal

Garage
Rock

Example 02 Rhythm

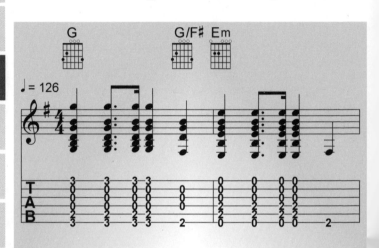

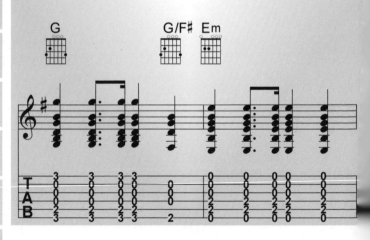

Blues Rock

Hard Rock

Glam Rock

Heavy Metal

Arena Rock

AOR Rock

Punk Rock

Grunge Rock

Indie Rock

Brit pop

Nu Metal

Garage Rock

Glam Rock

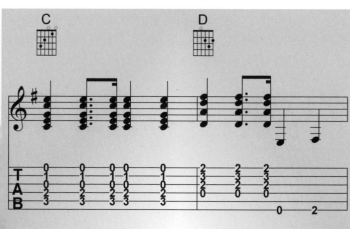

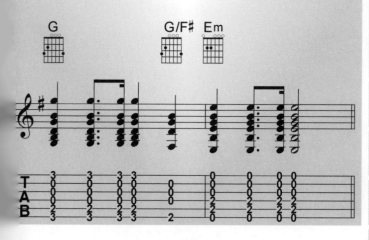

Blues Rock

Hard Rock

Glam Rock

Heavy Metal

Arena Rock

AOR Rock

Punk Rock

Grunge Rock

Indie Rock

Brit pop

Nu Metal

Garage Rock

Example 03 Rhythm

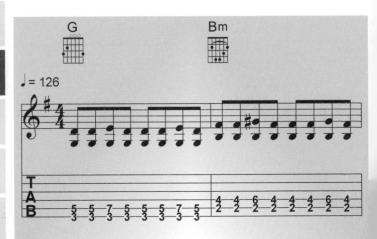

Glam Rock

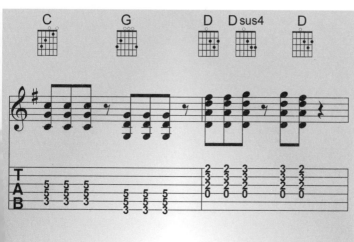

Blues Rock

Hard Rock

Glam Rock

Heavy Metal

Arena Rock

AOR Rock

Punk Rock

Grunge Rock

Indie Rock

Brit pop

Nu Metal

Garage Rock

Example 04 Rhythm

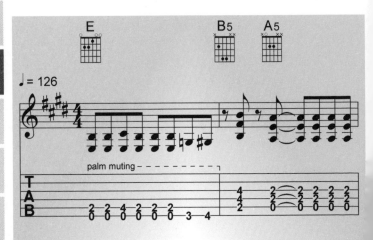

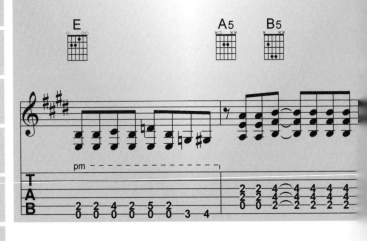

Glam Rock

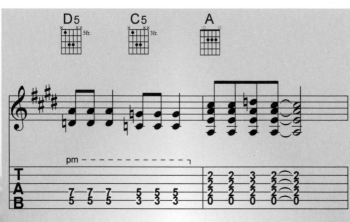

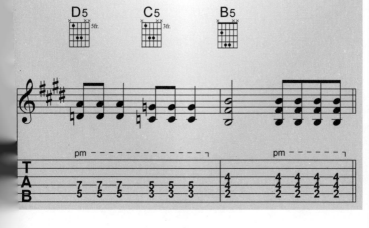

Blues Rock

Hard Rock

Glam Rock

Heavy Metal

Arena Rock

AOR Rock

Punk Rock

Grunge Rock

Indie Rock

Brit pop

Nu Metal

Garage Rock

Example 05 Riff

Blues
Rock

Hard
Rock

Glam
Rock

Heavy
Metal

Arena
Rock

AOR
Rock

Punk
Rock

Grunge
Rock

Indie
Rock

Brit
pop

Nu
Metal

Garage
Rock

With fuzzy dist.

Glam Rock

Blues
Rock

Hard
Rock

Glam
Rock

Heavy
Metal

Arena
Rock

AOR
Rock

Punk
Rock

Grunge
Rock

Indie
Rock

Brit
pop

Nu
Metal

Garage
Rock

Example 06 Riff

Glam Rock

Blues
Rock

Hard
Rock

Glam
Rock

Heavy
Metal

Arena
Rock

AOR
Rock

Punk
Rock

Grunge
Rock

Indie
Rock

Brit
pop

Nu
Metal

Garage
Rock

Example 07 Riff

Glam Rock

Blues Rock

Hard Rock

Glam Rock

Heavy Metal

Arena Rock

AOR Rock

Punk Rock

Grunge Rock

Indie Rock

Brit pop

Nu Metal

Garage Rock

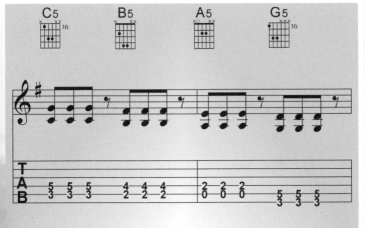

Example 08 Riff

Blues Rock

Hard Rock

Glam Rock

Heavy Metal

Arena Rock

AOR Rock

Punk Rock

Grunge Rock

Indie Rock

Brit pop

Nu Metal

Garage Rock

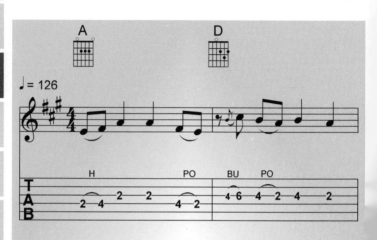

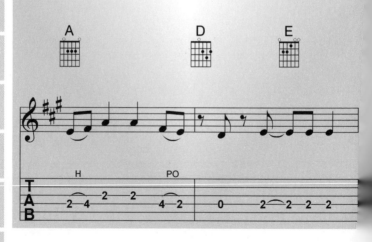

Glam Rock

Blues Rock

Hard Rock

Glam Rock

Heavy Metal

Arena Rock

AOR Rock

Punk Rock

Grunge Rock

Indie Rock

Brit pop

Nu Metal

Garage Rock

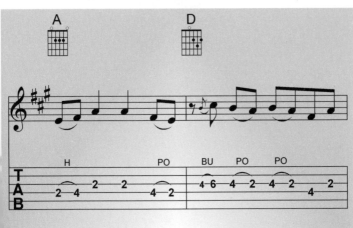

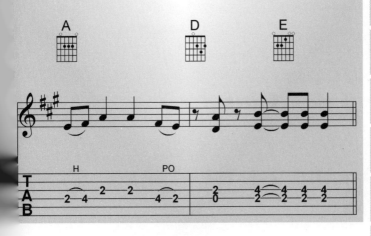

Example 09 Lead

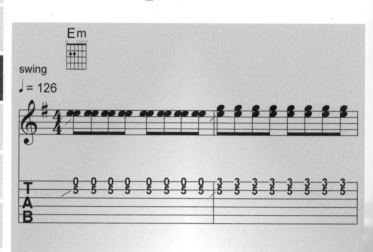

Glam Rock

Blues Rock

Hard Rock

Glam Rock

Heavy Metal

Arena Rock

AOR Rock

Punk Rock

Grunge Rock

Indie Rock

Brit pop

Nu Metal

Garage Rock

Example 10 Lead

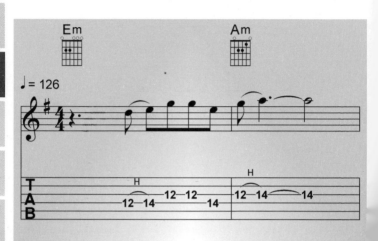

Glam Rock

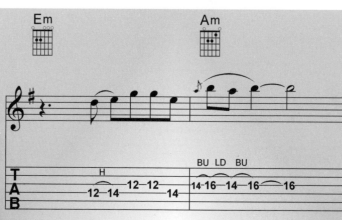

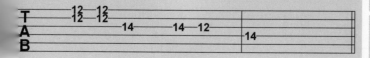

Blues Rock

Hard Rock

Glam Rock

Heavy Metal

Arena Rock

AOR Rock

Punk Rock

Grunge Rock

Indie Rock

Brit pop

Nu Metal

Garage Rock

Example 11 Lead

Glam Rock

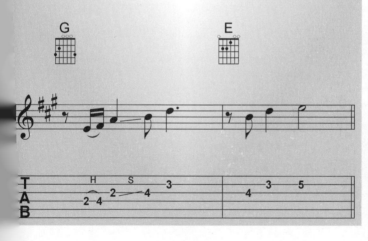

Blues Rock

Hard Rock

Glam Rock

Heavy Metal

Arena Rock

AOR Rock

Punk Rock

Grunge Rock

Indie Rock

Brit pop

Nu Metal

Garage Rock

Example 12 Lead

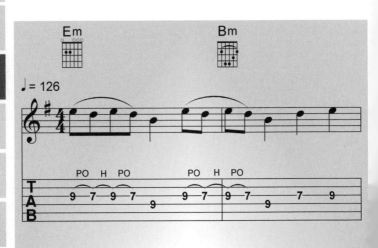

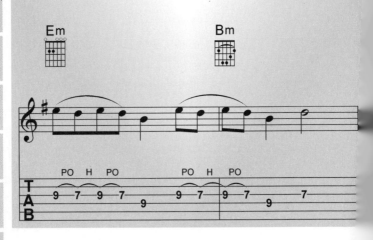

Glam Rock

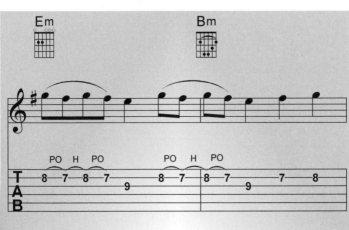

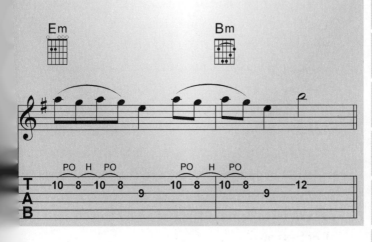

Blues Rock

Hard Rock

Glam Rock

Heavy Metal

Arena Rock

AOR Rock

Punk Rock

Grunge Rock

Indie Rock

Brit pop

Nu Metal

Garage Rock

Blues
Rock

Hard
Rock

Glam
Rock

Heavy
Metal

Arena
Rock

AOR
Rock

Punk
Rock

Grunge
Rock

Indie
Rock

Brit
pop

Nu
Metal

Garage
Rock

Heavy Metal

The dividing line between hard rock and heavy metal may sometimes be difficult to establish. The term heavy metal is generally reckoned to have originated in Steppenwolf's 1969 hit 'Born To Be Wild', which refers to 'heavy metal thunder'.

Certainly, hard rock increased the proportion of music to lyrics, and the music was often reduced to thundering riffs rather than thoughtful chord progressions. Lyrically, black magic and sword and sorcery were popular subjects, this often reflected in ever more complex album cover art. Uriah Heep, Deep Purple, Judas Priest and particularly Black Sabbath proved long lasting exponents. In the early Eighties a new wave of heavy metal band appeared as the supergroups of the previous decade had split or decamped to the States. Iron Maiden, Saxon, Def Leppard and the like formed to re-establish a grass-roots live circuit. Maiden proved themselves able successors to Deep Purple as the world's most popular metal band, while Kiss found an audience all of their own.

Blues
Rock

Hard
Rock

Glam
Rock

**Heavy
Metal**

Arena
Rock

AOR
Rock

Punk
Rock

Grunge
Rock

Indie
Rock

Brit
pop

Nu
Metal

Garage
Rock

Example 01 Rhythm

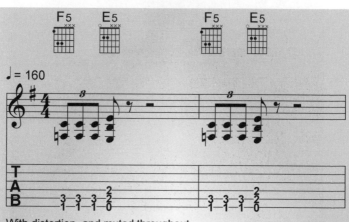

With distortion, and muted throughout.

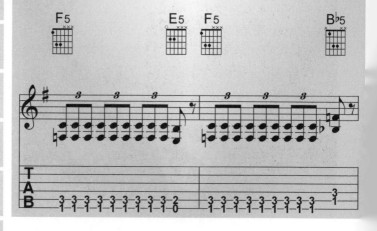

Heavy Metal

Blues Rock

Hard Rock

Glam Rock

Heavy Metal

Arena Rock

AOR Rock

Punk Rock

Grunge Rock

Indie Rock

Brit pop

Nu Metal

Garage Rock

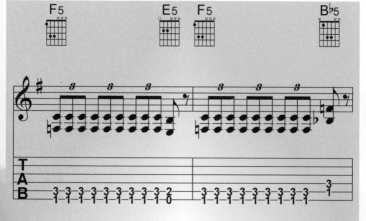

Example 02 Rhythm

Blues Rock

Hard Rock

Glam Rock

Heavy Metal

Arena Rock

AOR Rock

Punk Rock

Grunge Rock

Indie Rock

Brit pop

Nu Metal

Garage Rock

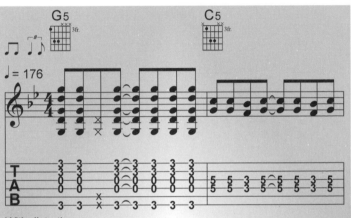

With distortion.

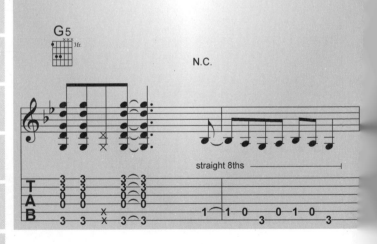

Heavy Metal

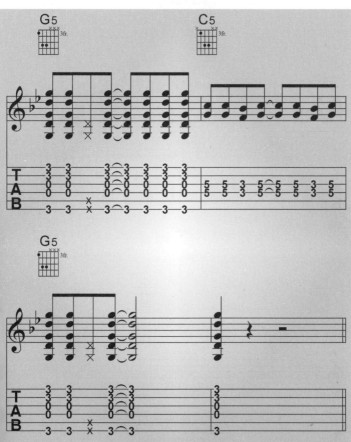

Blues
Rock

Hard
Rock

Glam
Rock

**Heavy
Metal**

Arena
Rock

AOR
Rock

Punk
Rock

Grunge
Rock

Indie
Rock

Brit
pop

Nu
Metal

Garage
Rock

Example 03 Rhythm

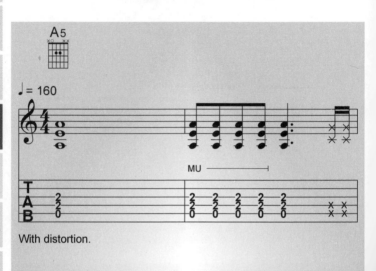

With distortion.

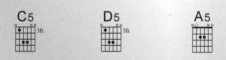

Heavy Metal

Blues
Rock

Hard
Rock

Glam
Rock

**Heavy
Metal**

Arena
Rock

AOR
Rock

Punk
Rock

Grunge
Rock

Indie
Rock

Brit
pop

Nu
Metal

Garage
Rock

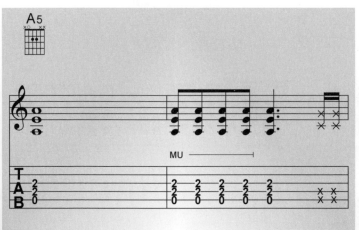

A5

MU

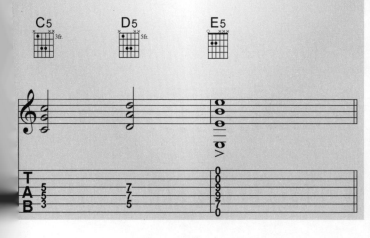

C5   D5   E5

Example 04 Rhythm

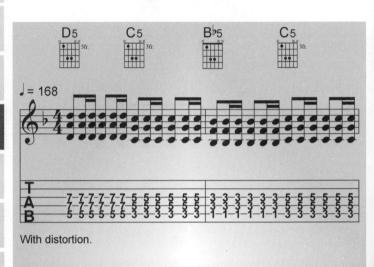

With distortion.

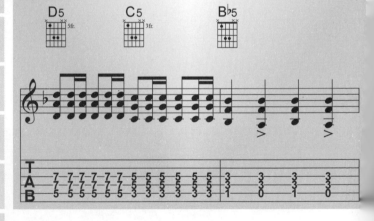

Heavy Metal

Blues Rock

Hard Rock

Glam Rock

Heavy Metal

Arena Rock

AOR Rock

Punk Rock

Grunge Rock

Indie Rock

Brit pop

Nu Metal

Garage Rock

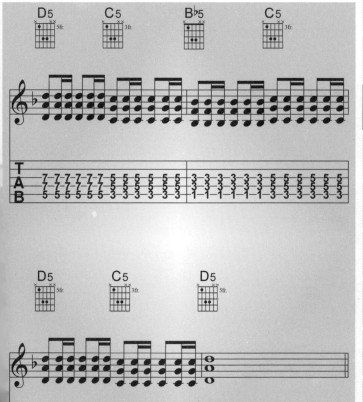

Example 05 Riff

Blues
Rock

Hard
Rock

Glam
Rock

Heavy
Metal

Arena
Rock

AOR
Rock

Punk
Rock

Grunge
Rock

Indie
Rock

Brit
pop

Nu
Metal

Garage
Rock

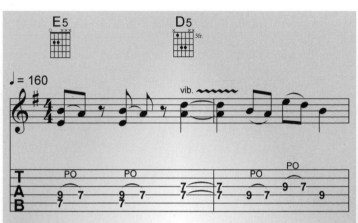

With distortion.

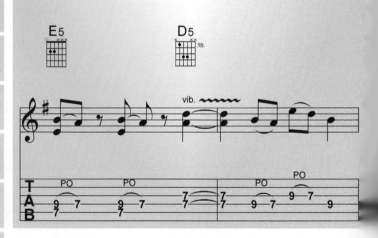

Heavy Metal

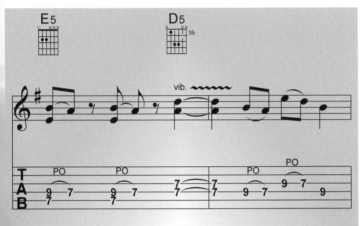

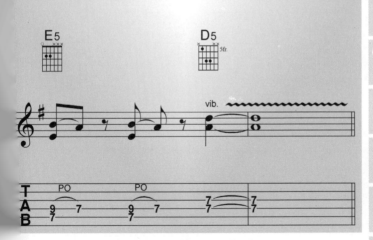

Blues Rock

Hard Rock

Glam Rock

Heavy Metal

Arena Rock

AOR Rock

Punk Rock

Grunge Rock

Indie Rock

Brit pop

Nu Metal

Garage Rock

Example 06 Riff

Blues Rock
Hard Rock
Glam Rock
Heavy Metal
Arena Rock
AOR Rock
Punk Rock
Grunge Rock
Indie Rock
Brit pop
Nu Metal
Garage Rock

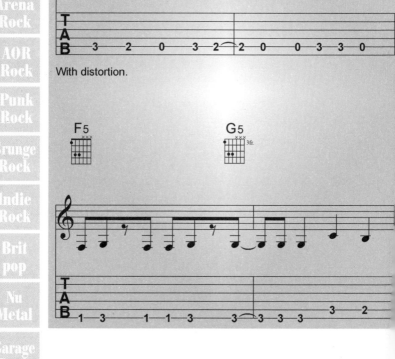

With distortion.

Heavy Metal

Blues
Rock

Hard
Rock

Glam
Rock

Heavy
Metal

Arena
Rock

AOR
Rock

Punk
Rock

Grunge
Rock

Indie
Rock

Brit
pop

Nu
Metal

Garage
Rock

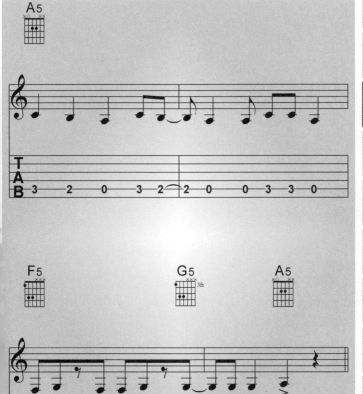

Example 07 Riff

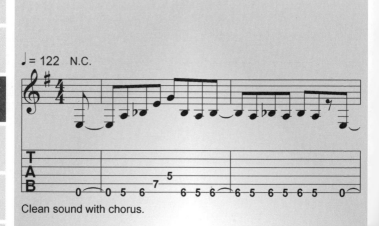

Clean sound with chorus.

Heavy Metal

Blues Rock

Hard Rock

Glam Rock

Heavy Metal

Arena Rock

AOR Rock

Punk Rock

Grunge Rock

Indie Rock

Brit pop

Nu Metal

Garage Rock

Example 08 Riff

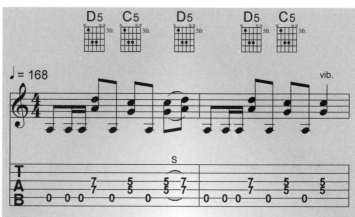

With distortion.

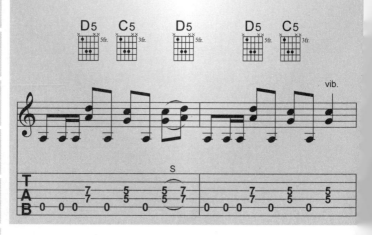

Heavy Metal

Blues
Rock

Hard
Rock

Glam
Rock

**Heavy
Metal**

Arena
Rock

AOR
Rock

Punk
Rock

Grunge
Rock

Indie
Rock

Brit
pop

Nu
Metal

Garage
Rock

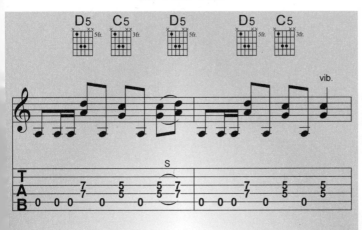

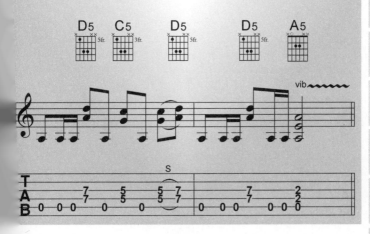

Example 09 Lead

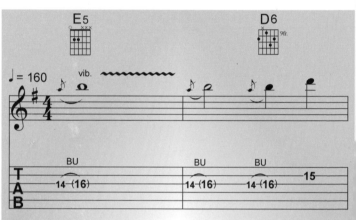

With distortion.

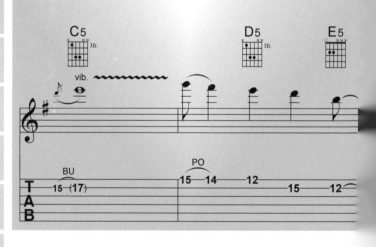

Heavy Metal

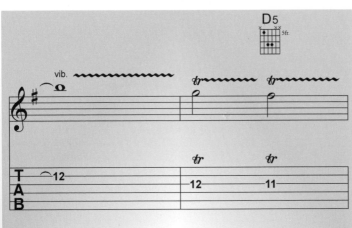

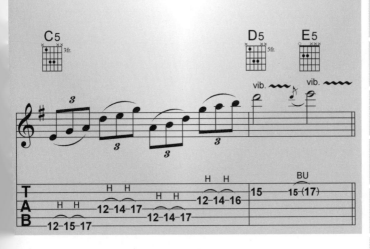

Blues
Rock

Hard
Rock

Glam
Rock

**Heavy
Metal**

Arena
Rock

AOR
Rock

Punk
Rock

Grunge
Rock

Indie
Rock

Brit
pop

Nu
Metal

Garage
Rock

Example 10 Lead

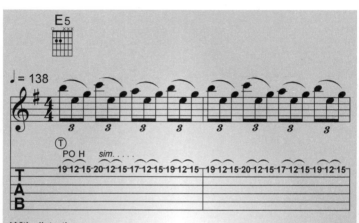

With distortion.

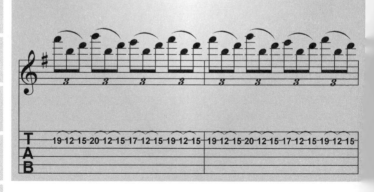

Blues Rock

Hard Rock

Glam Rock

Heavy Metal

Arena Rock

AOR Rock

Punk Rock

Grunge Rock

Indie Rock

Brit pop

Nu Metal

Garage Rock

Heavy Metal

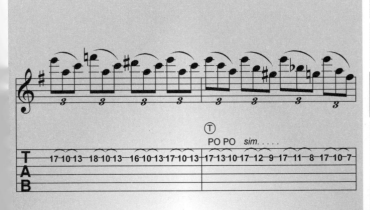

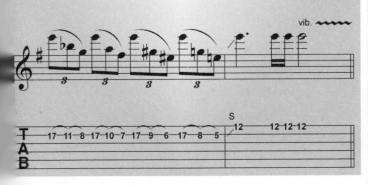

Blues Rock

Hard Rock

Glam Rock

Heavy Metal

Arena Rock

AOR Rock

Punk Rock

Grunge Rock

Indie Rock

Brit pop

Nu Metal

Garage Rock

Example 11 Lead

Blues
Rock

Hard
Rock

Glam
Rock

**Heavy
Metal**

Arena
Rock

AOR
Rock

Punk
Rock

Grunge
Rock

Indie
Rock

Brit
pop

Nu
Metal

Garage
Rock

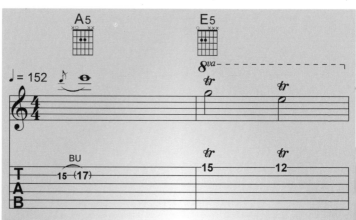

With distortion.

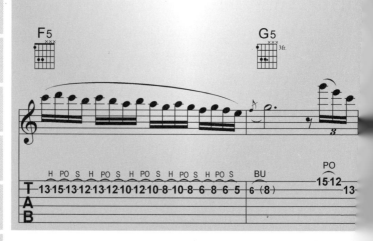

Heavy Metal

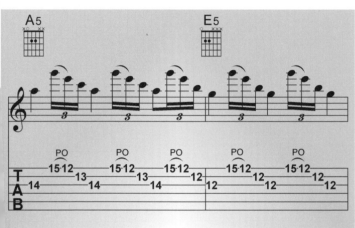

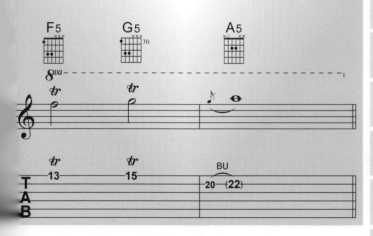

Blues Rock

Hard Rock

Glam Rock

Heavy Metal

Arena Rock

AOR Rock

Punk Rock

Grunge Rock

Indie Rock

Brit pop

Nu Metal

Garage Rock

Example 12 Lead

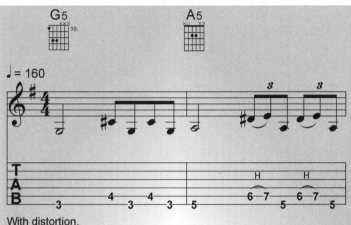

With distortion.

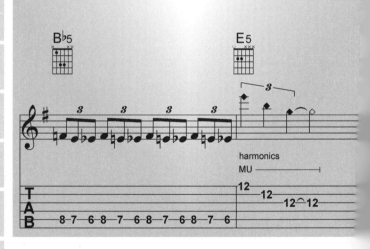

Heavy Metal

Blues
Rock

Hard
Rock

Glam
Rock

**Heavy
Metal**

Arena
Rock

AOR
Rock

Punk
Rock

Grunge
Rock

Indie
Rock

Brit
pop

Nu
Metal

Garage
Rock

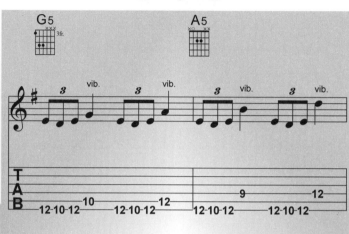

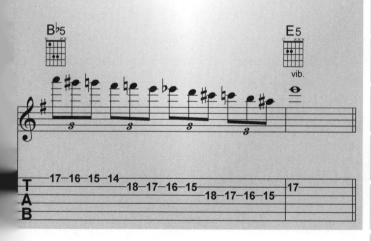

Blues
Rock

Hard
Rock

Glam
Rock

Heavy
Metal

Arena
Rock

AOR
Rock

Punk
Rock

Grunge
Rock

Indie
Rock

Brit
pop

Nu
Metal

Garage
Rock

Arena Rock

Arena rock was played by any band that could attract enough of an audience to fill a sports stadium. So riffs had to be able to hit the person in row Z, the cheap seats. Volume was important of course but Queen's Brian May and U2's the Edge both used effects to compensate for the fact that they were the sole melodic instrument in a three-piece set-up. Delay was a major part of this armoury, with arpeggiated picking particularly effective.

Mark Knopfler and Joe Perry, of Dire Straits and Aerosmith respectively, boasted high technique and a penchant for snappy, memorable riffs. Knopfler graduated from the subtle fingerpicking of 'Sultans Of Swing' to the bludgeoning power chords of (the admittedly tongue in cheek) 'Money For Nothing', while Perry supplied updated versions of the time-honoured blues riff. The re-formed Police also feature as arena rockers, Andy Summers supplying blankets of effects-laden tone from his Telecaster.

Blues
Rock

Hard
Rock

Glam
Rock

Heavy
Metal

**Arena
Rock**

AOR
Rock

Punk
Rock

Grunge
Rock

Indie
Rock

Brit
pop

Nu
Metal

Garage
Rock

Example 01 Rhythm

Arena Rock

Blues Rock

Hard Rock

Glam Rock

Heavy Metal

Arena Rock

AOR Rock

Punk Rock

Grunge Rock

Indie Rock

Brit pop

Nu Metal

Garage Rock

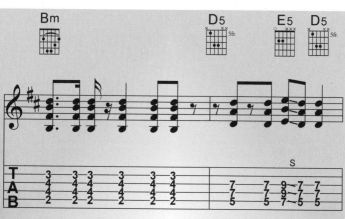

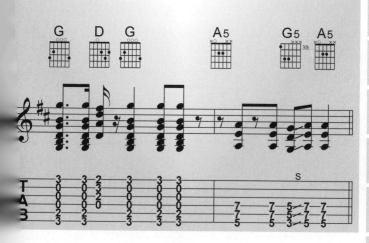

Example 02 Rhythm

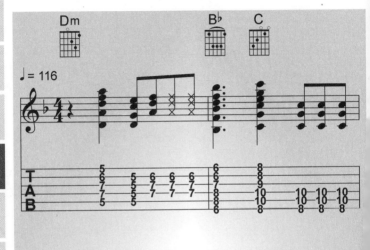

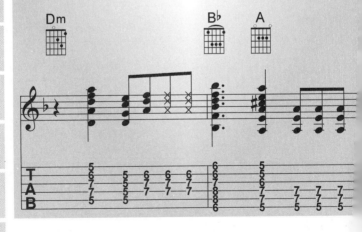

Arena Rock

Blues Rock

Hard Rock

Glam Rock

Heavy Metal

Arena Rock

AOR Rock

Punk Rock

Grunge Rock

Indie Rock

Brit pop

Nu Metal

Garage Rock

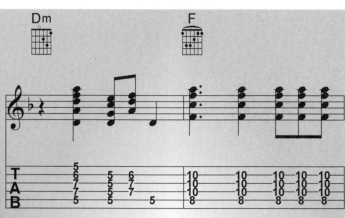

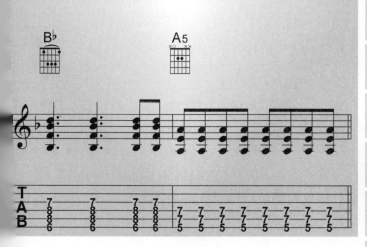

Example 03 Rhythm

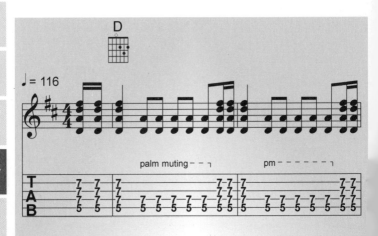

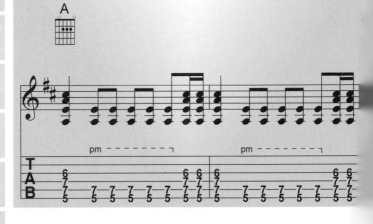

Arena Rock

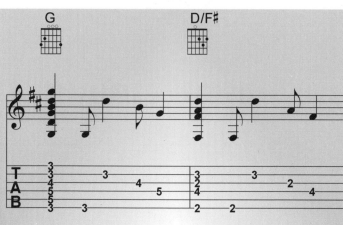

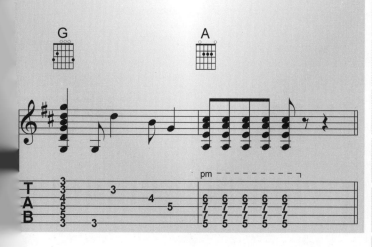

Blues Rock

Hard Rock

Glam Rock

Heavy Metal

Arena Rock

AOR Rock

Punk Rock

Grunge Rock

Indie Rock

Brit pop

Nu Metal

Garage Rock

Example 04 Rhythm

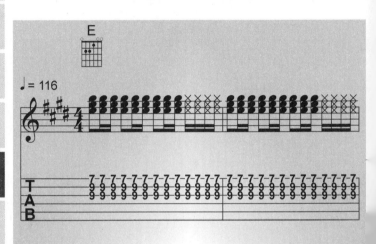

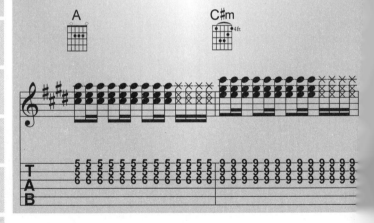

Arena Rock

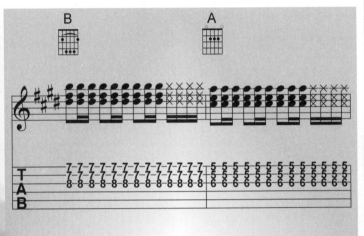

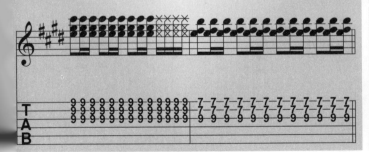

Blues
Rock

Hard
Rock

Glam
Rock

Heavy
Metal

Arena
Rock

AOR
Rock

Punk
Rock

Grunge
Rock

Indie
Rock

Brit
pop

Nu
Metal

Garage
Rock

Example 05 Riff

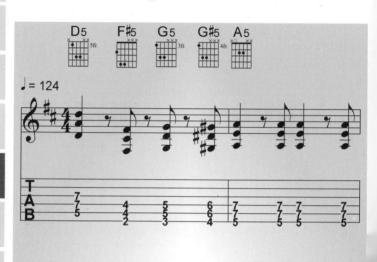

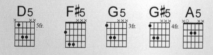

Arena Rock

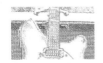

Blues Rock

Hard Rock

Glam Rock

Heavy Metal

Arena Rock

AOR Rock

Punk Rock

Grunge Rock

Indie Rock

Brit pop

Nu Metal

Garage Rock

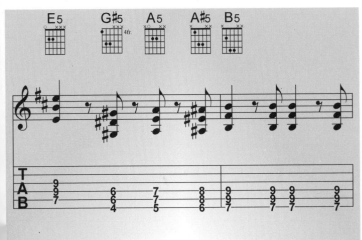

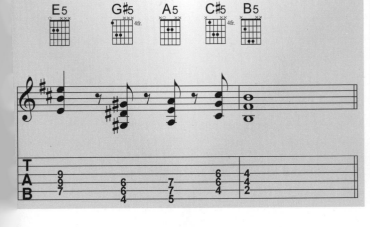

Example 06 Riff

Blues Rock
Hard Rock
Glam Rock
Heavy Metal
Arena Rock
AOR Rock
Punk Rock
Grunge Rock
Indie Rock
Brit pop
Nu Metal
Garage Rock

Arena Rock

Blues
Rock

Hard
Rock

Glam
Rock

Heavy
Metal

Arena
Rock

AOR
Rock

Punk
Rock

Grunge
Rock

Indie
Rock

Brit
pop

Nu
Metal

Garage
Rock

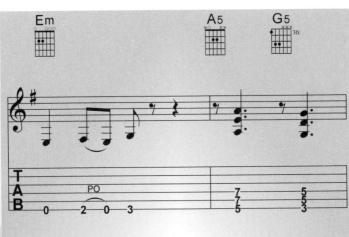

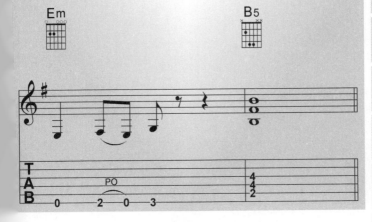

Example 07 Riff

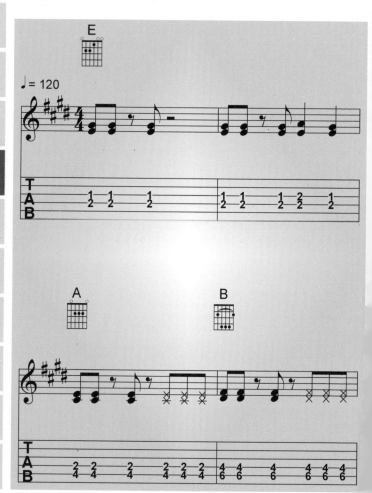

Arena Rock

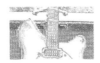

Blues Rock

Hard Rock

Glam Rock

Heavy Metal

Arena Rock

AOR Rock

Punk Rock

Grunge Rock

Indie Rock

Brit pop

Nu Metal

Garage Rock

175

Example 08 Riff

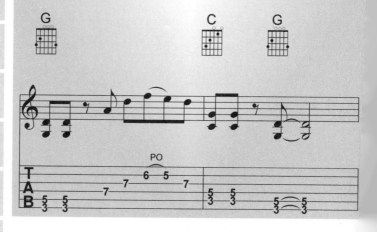

Blues Rock

Hard Rock

Glam Rock

Heavy Metal

Arena Rock

AOR Rock

Punk Rock

Grunge Rock

Indie Rock

Brit pop

Nu Metal

Garage Rock

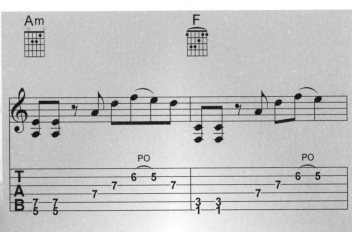

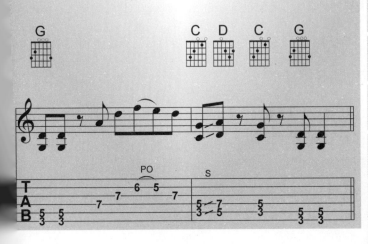

Example 09 Lead

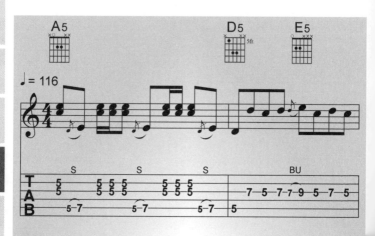

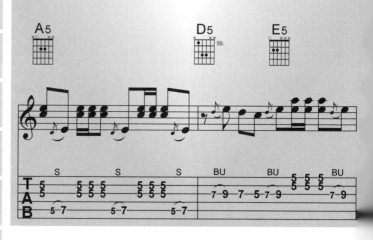

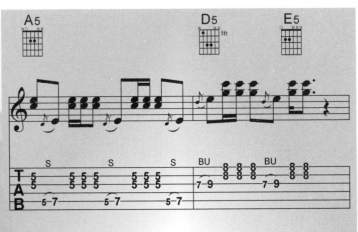

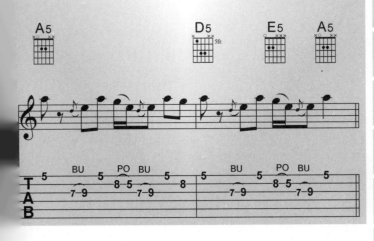

Blues Rock

Hard Rock

Glam Rock

Heavy Metal

Arena Rock

AOR Rock

Punk Rock

Grunge Rock

Indie Rock

Brit pop

Nu Metal

Garage Rock

Example 10 Lead

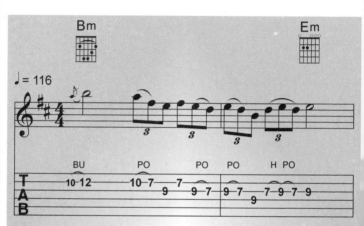

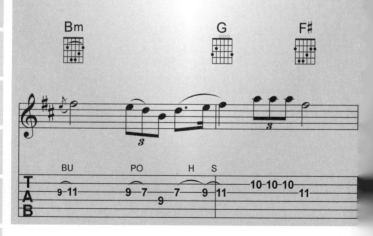

Arena Rock

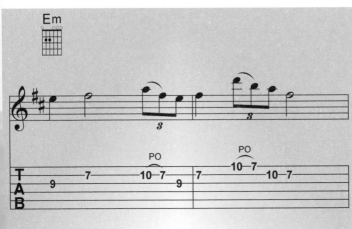

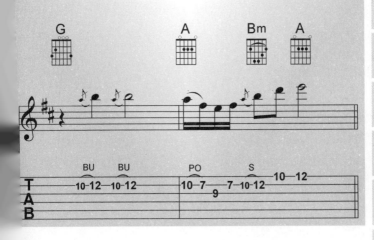

Blues Rock

Hard Rock

Glam Rock

Heavy Metal

Arena Rock

AOR Rock

Punk Rock

Grunge Rock

Indie Rock

Brit pop

Nu Metal

Garage Rock

Example 11 Lead

Blues Rock

Hard Rock

Glam Rock

Heavy Metal

Arena Rock

AOR Rock

Punk Rock

Grunge Rock

Indie Rock

Brit pop

Nu Metal

Garage Rock

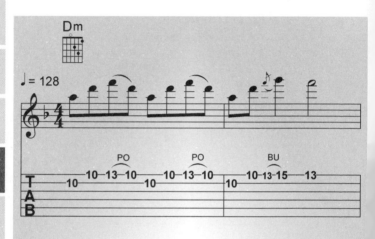

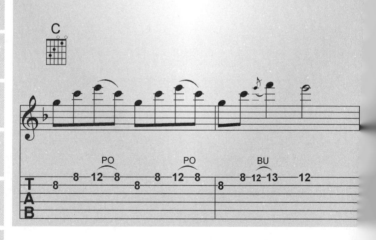

Arena Rock

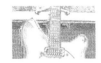

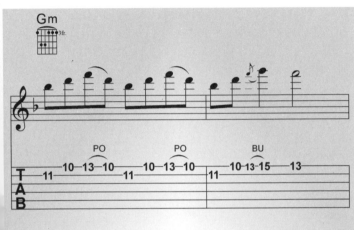

Blues Rock

Hard Rock

Glam Rock

Heavy Metal

Arena Rock

AOR Rock

Punk Rock

Grunge Rock

Indie Rock

Brit pop

Nu Metal

Garage Rock

Example 12 Lead

Blues Rock

Hard Rock

Glam Rock

Heavy Metal

Arena Rock

AOR Rock

Punk Rock

Grunge Rock

Indie Rock

Brit pop

Nu Metal

Garage Rock

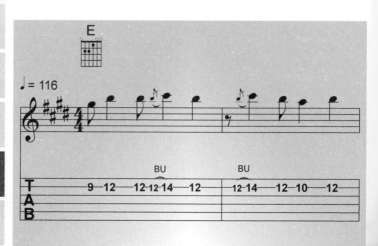

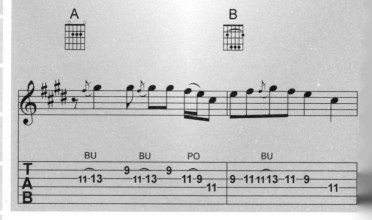

Arena Rock

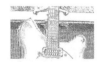

Blues Rock

Hard Rock

Glam Rock

Heavy Metal

Arena Rock

AOR Rock

Punk Rock

Grunge Rock

Indie Rock

Brit pop

Nu Metal

Garage Rock

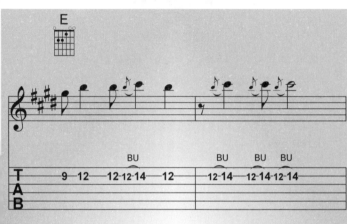

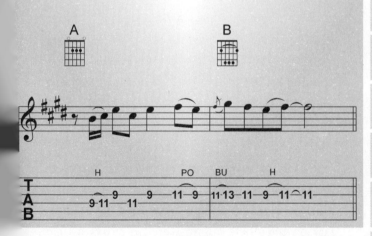

Blues Rock

Hard Rock

Glam Rock

Heavy Metal

Arena Rock

AOR Rock

Punk Rock

Grunge Rock

Indie Rock

Brit pop

Nu Metal

Garage Rock

AOR Rock

If one sound exemplified Seventies soft rock, or adult-oriented rock as most people prefer to call it, it would be the arpeggiated Les Paul guitar that propelled Boston's 1976 single 'More Than A Feeling' to multi-platinum status, taking their eponymous debut album with it.

Many AOR bands varied the focus with added instrumentation. Hence Chicago's 'gimmick' was an accomplished horn section that played on more or less every number and was integral to the group, whereas Foreigner, while starting out as basic heavy guitar rockers found most success when they based their songs on keyboard riffs, in numbers such as 'Waiting For A Girl Like You'. This notwithstanding the fact that their main songwriter and leader, Mick Jones, was a guitarist.

Toto, REO Speedwagon and Styx were successful in the same musical vein. Toto's Steve Lukather was a much-in-demand session man used by Michael Jackson and others, but for every guitar-based 'Hold The Line' was a synth-drenched 'Africa'.

Blues
Rock

Hard
Rock

Glam
Rock

Heavy
Metal

Arena
Rock

**AOR
Rock**

Punk
Rock

Grunge
Rock

Indie
Rock

Brit
pop

Nu
Metal

Garage
Rock

Example 01 Rhythm

AOR Rock

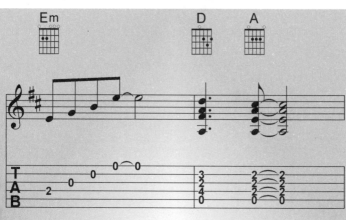

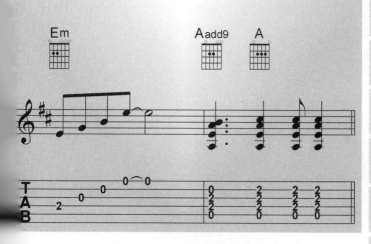

Blues Rock

Hard Rock

Glam Rock

Heavy Metal

Arena Rock

AOR Rock

Punk Rock

Grunge Rock

Indie Rock

Brit pop

Nu Metal

Garage Rock

Example 02 Rhythm

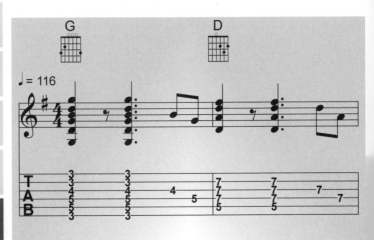

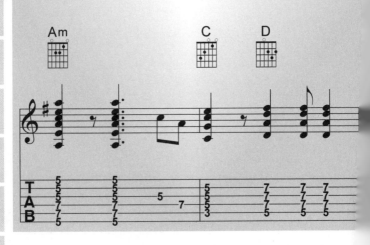

AOR Rock

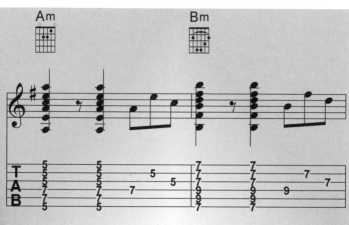

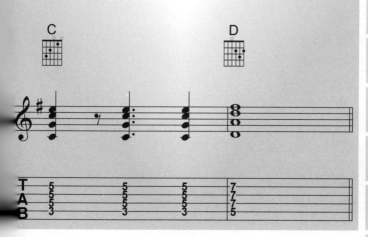

Blues Rock

Hard Rock

Glam Rock

Heavy Metal

Arena Rock

AOR Rock

Punk Rock

Grunge Rock

Indie Rock

Brit pop

Nu Metal

Garage Rock

Example 03 Rhythm

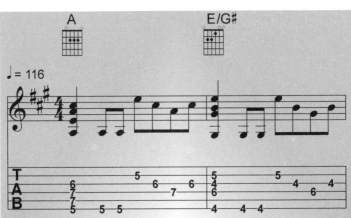

Palm mute single notes throughout.

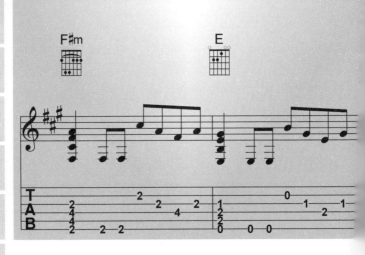

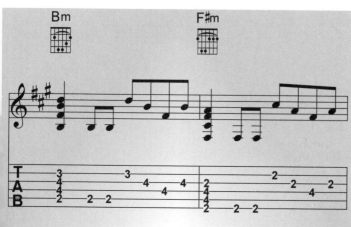

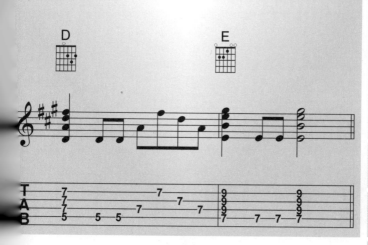

Blues Rock

Hard Rock

Glam Rock

Heavy Metal

Arena Rock

AOR Rock

Punk Rock

Grunge Rock

Indie Rock

Brit pop

Nu Metal

Garage Rock

Example 04 Rhythm

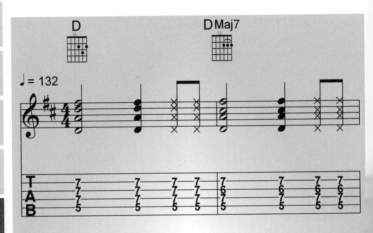

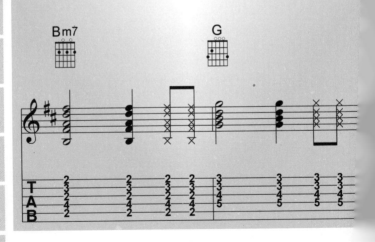

AOR Rock

Blues Rock

Hard Rock

Glam Rock

Heavy Metal

Arena Rock

AOR Rock

Punk Rock

Grunge Rock

Indie Rock

Brit pop

Nu Metal

Garage Rock

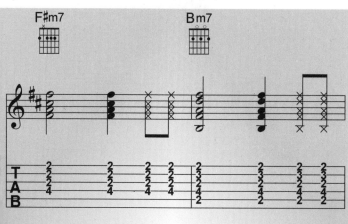

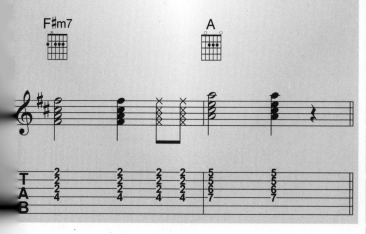

Example 05 Riff

Blues
Rock

Hard
Rock

Glam
Rock

Heavy
Metal

Arena
Rock

**AOR
Rock**

Punk
Rock

Grunge
Rock

Indie
Rock

Brit
pop

Nu
Metal

Garage
Rock

AOR Rock

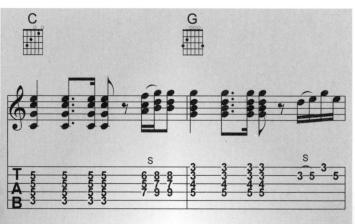

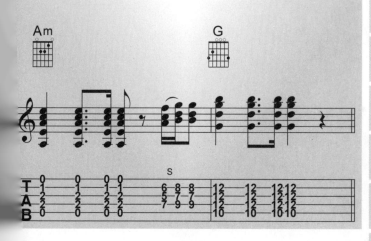

Blues Rock

Hard Rock

Glam Rock

Heavy Metal

Arena Rock

AOR Rock

Punk Rock

Grunge Rock

Indie Rock

Brit pop

Nu Metal

Garage Rock

Example 06 Riff

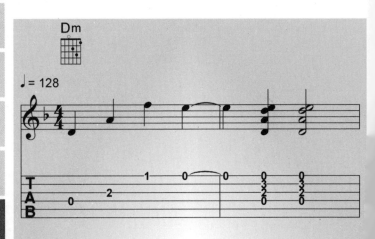

AOR Rock

Blues Rock

Hard Rock

Glam Rock

Heavy Metal

Arena Rock

AOR Rock

Punk Rock

Grunge Rock

Indie Rock

Brit pop

Nu Metal

Garage Rock

F Maj7

Am

Example 07 Riff

AOR Rock

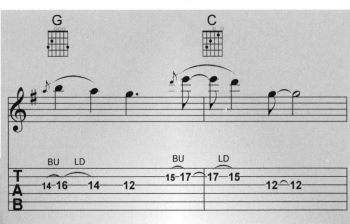

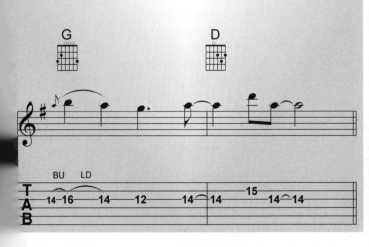

Blues Rock

Hard Rock

Glam Rock

Heavy Metal

Arena Rock

AOR Rock

Punk Rock

Grunge Rock

Indie Rock

Brit pop

Nu Metal

Garage Rock

Example 08 Riff

Blues Rock

Hard Rock

Glam Rock

Heavy Metal

Arena Rock

AOR Rock

Punk Rock

Grunge Rock

Indie Rock

Brit pop

Nu Metal

Garage Rock

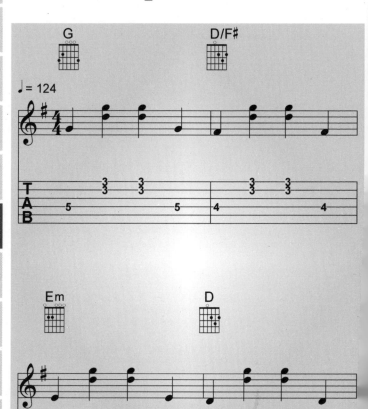

AOR Rock

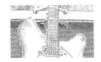

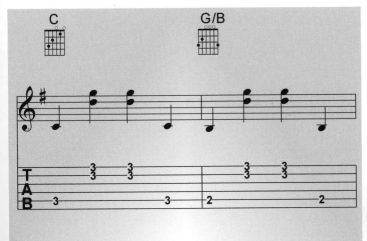

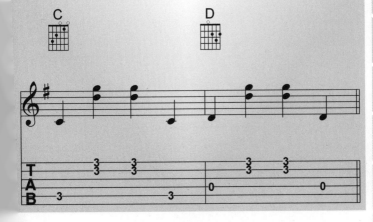

Blues Rock

Hard Rock

Glam Rock

Heavy Metal

Arena Rock

AOR Rock

Punk Rock

Grunge Rock

Indie Rock

Brit pop

Nu Metal

Garage Rock

Example 09 Lead

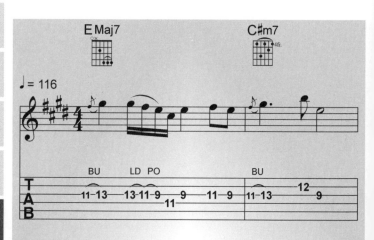

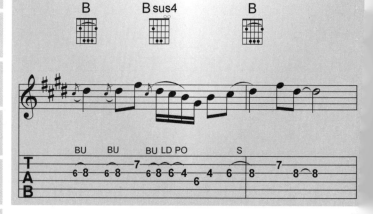

AOR Rock

Blues Rock

Hard Rock

Glam Rock

Heavy Metal

Arena Rock

AOR Rock

Punk Rock

Grunge Rock

Indie Rock

Brit pop

Nu Metal

Garage Rock

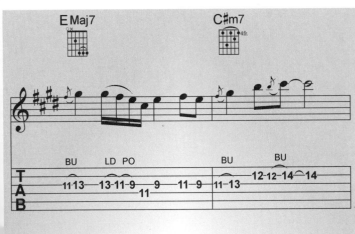

205

Example 10 Lead

AOR Rock

Blues Rock

Hard Rock

Glam Rock

Heavy Metal

Arena Rock

AOR Rock

Punk Rock

Grunge Rock

Indie Rock

Brit pop

Nu Metal

Garage Rock

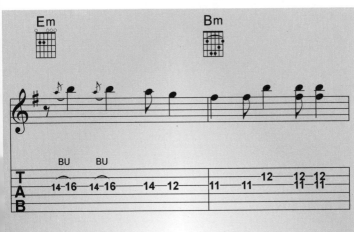

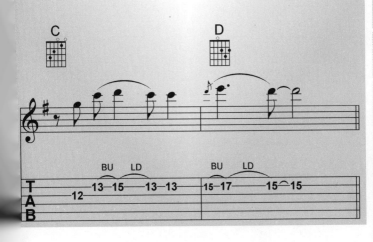

Example 11 Lead

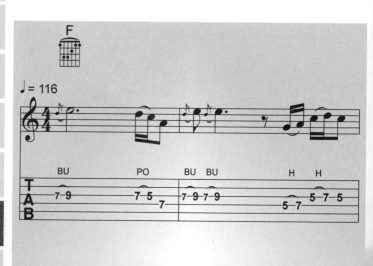

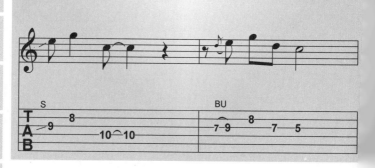

AOR Rock

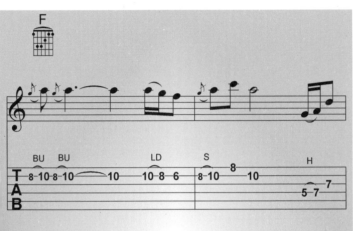

Blues Rock

Hard Rock

Glam Rock

Heavy Metal

Arena Rock

AOR Rock

Punk Rock

Grunge Rock

Indie Rock

Brit pop

Nu Metal

Garage Rock

Example 12 Lead

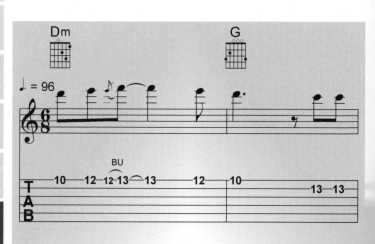

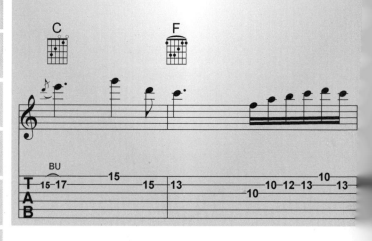

AOR Rock

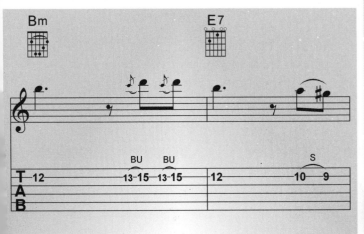

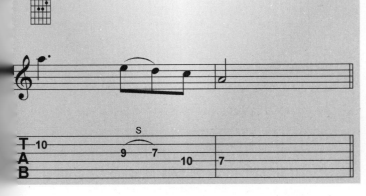

Blues Rock

Hard Rock

Glam Rock

Heavy Metal

Arena Rock

AOR Rock

Punk Rock

Grunge Rock

Indie Rock

Brit pop

Nu Metal

Garage Rock

Blues
Rock

Hard
Rock

Glam
Rock

Heavy
Metal

Arena
Rock

AOR
Rock

Punk
Rock

Grunge
Rock

Indie
Rock

Brit
pop

Nu
Metal

Garage
Rock

Punk Rock

When TV host Bob Harris condemned the New York Dolls as 'mock rock' in 1973, little did he know that three years later the punk revolution would see that band as a template. Johnny Thunders' rudimentary yet exciting style, playing a basic one-pickup Gibson loud and clean, relied on natural distortion: 'Just plug in, turn up and spank it' was his motto.

It is said that the powerful guitar work on the Sex Pistols' 1977 album Never Mind The Bollocks was played by studio musician Chris Spedding rather than the group's own Steve Jones. Whatever the truth, it is the power chords of the rhythm contrasted with some fairly basic two-note soloing that defines the punk style. Johnny Ramone was famous for not playing solos at all, but if you had to then minimal was best. The Clash's double punk punch of Joe Strummer (rhythm) and Mick Jones (lead) was more conventional. Amplifier-wise, mid and treble were wound to the maximum, using the transistor gain channel or just sheer volume to obtain distortion and excitement.

Blues
Rock

Hard
Rock

Glam
Rock

Heavy
Metal

Arena
Rock

AOR
Rock

Punk
Rock

Grunge
Rock

Indie
Rock

Brit
pop

Nu
Metal

Garage
Rock

Example 01 Rhythm

Blues Rock

Hard Rock

Glam Rock

Heavy Metal

Arena Rock

AOR Rock

Punk Rock

Grunge Rock

Indie Rock

Brit pop

Nu Metal

Garage Rock

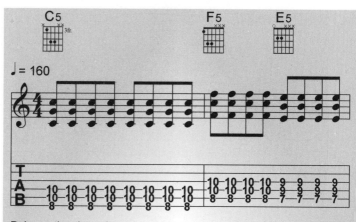

Palm muting throughout.

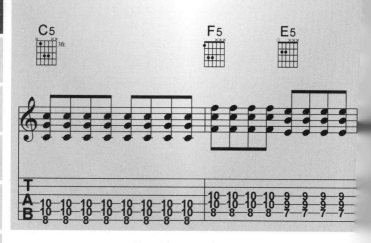

Punk Rock

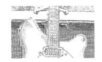

Blues Rock

Hard Rock

Glam Rock

Heavy Metal

Arena Rock

AOR Rock

Punk Rock

Grunge Rock

Indie Rock

Brit pop

Nu Metal

Garage Rock

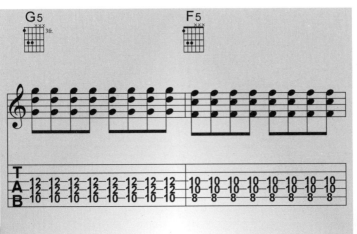

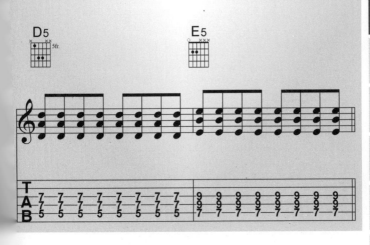

Example 02 Rhythm

Blues
Rock

Hard
Rock

Glam
Rock

Heavy
Metal

Arena
Rock

AOR
Rock

Punk
Rock

Grunge
Rock

Indie
Rock

Brit
pop

Nu
Metal

Garage
Rock

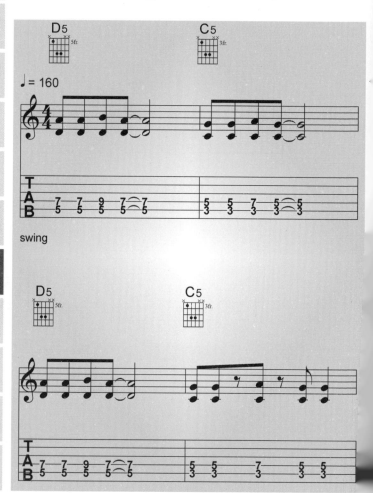

Punk Rock

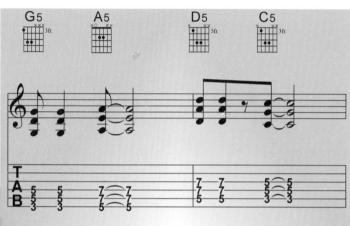

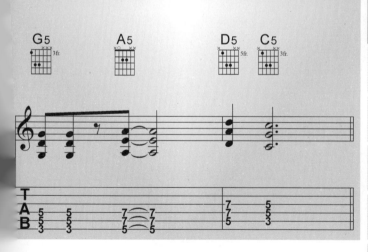

Blues
Rock

Hard
Rock

Glam
Rock

Heavy
Metal

Arena
Rock

AOR
Rock

Punk
Rock

Grunge
Rock

Indie
Rock

Brit
pop

Nu
Metal

Garage
Rock

Example 03 Rhythm

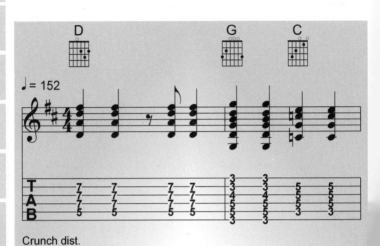

Crunch dist.

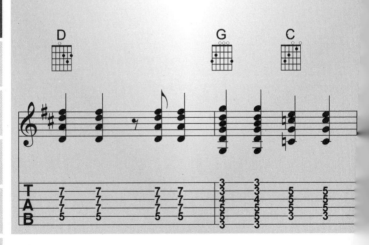

Punk Rock

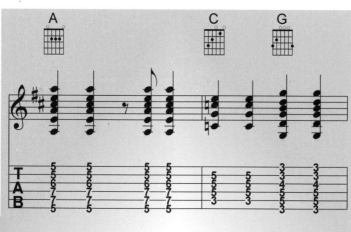

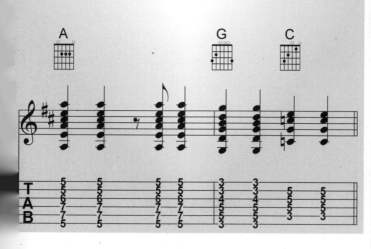

Blues Rock

Hard Rock

Glam Rock

Heavy Metal

Arena Rock

AOR Rock

Punk Rock

Grunge Rock

Indie Rock

Brit pop

Nu Metal

Garage Rock

Example 04 Rhythm

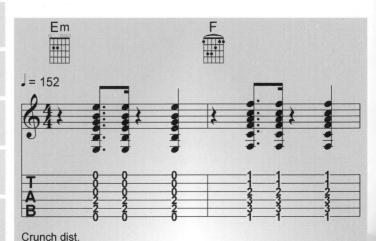

Crunch dist.

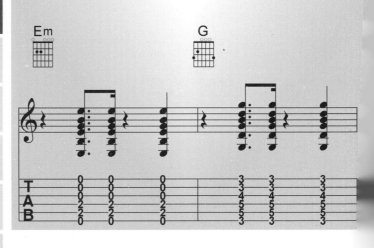

Punk Rock

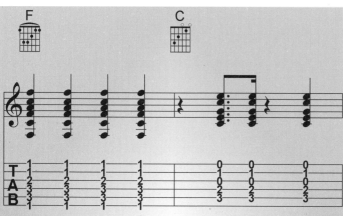

Blues Rock

Hard Rock

Glam Rock

Heavy Metal

Arena Rock

AOR Rock

Punk Rock

Grunge Rock

Indie Rock

Brit pop

Nu Metal

Garage Rock

Example 05 Riff

Blues Rock

Hard Rock

Glam Rock

Heavy Metal

Arena Rock

AOR Rock

Punk Rock

Grunge Rock

Indie Rock

Brit pop

Nu Metal

Garage Rock

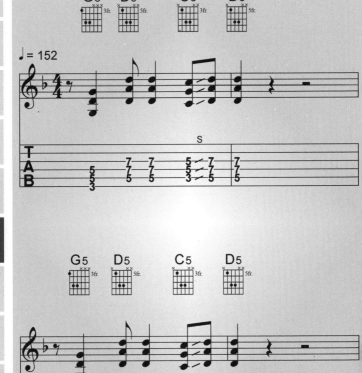

Punk Rock

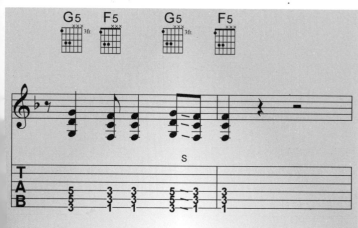

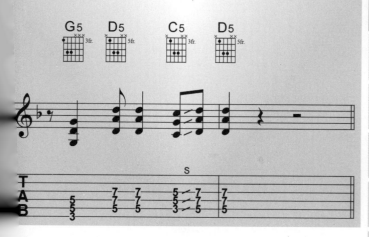

Blues Rock

Hard Rock

Glam Rock

Heavy Metal

Arena Rock

AOR Rock

Punk Rock

Grunge Rock

Indie Rock

Brit pop

Nu Metal

Garage Rock

Example 06 Riff

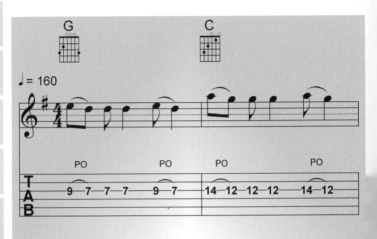

Blues Rock

Hard Rock

Glam Rock

Heavy Metal

Arena Rock

AOR Rock

Punk Rock

Grunge Rock

Indie Rock

Brit pop

Nu Metal

Garage Rock

Punk Rock

Blues
Rock

Hard
Rock

Glam
Rock

Heavy
Metal

Arena
Rock

AOR
Rock

Punk
Rock

Grunge
Rock

Indie
Rock

Brit
pop

Nu
Metal

Garage
Rock

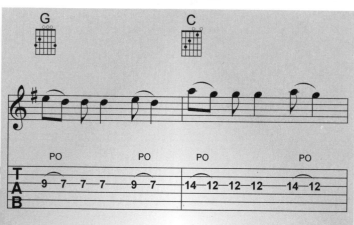

225

Example 07 Riff

Blues
Rock

Hard
Rock

Glam
Rock

Heavy
Metal

Arena
Rock

AOR
Rock

Punk
Rock

Grunge
Rock

Indie
Rock

Brit
pop

Nu
Metal

Garage
Rock

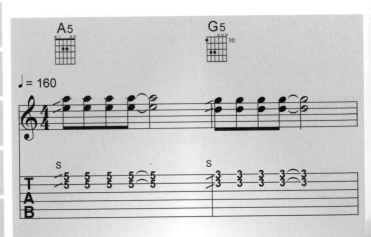

Punk Rock

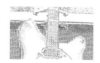

Blues Rock

Hard Rock

Glam Rock

Heavy Metal

Arena Rock

AOR Rock

Punk Rock

Grunge Rock

Indie Rock

Brit pop

Nu Metal

Garage Rock

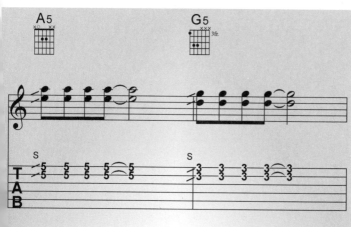

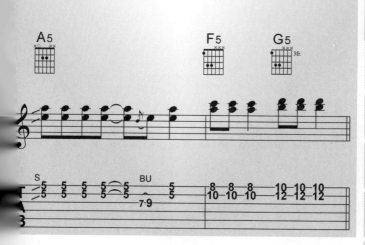

Example 08 Riff

Punk Rock

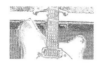

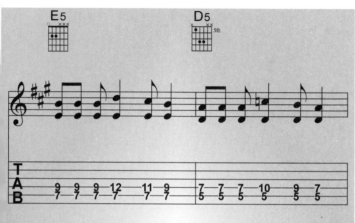

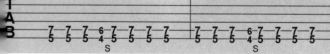

Blues Rock

Hard Rock

Glam Rock

Heavy Metal

Arena Rock

AOR Rock

Punk Rock

Grunge Rock

Indie Rock

Brit pop

Nu Metal

Garage Rock

Example 09 Lead

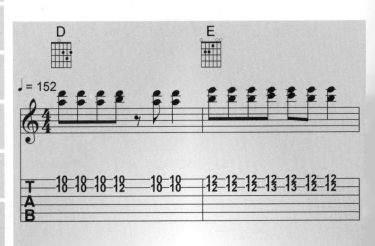

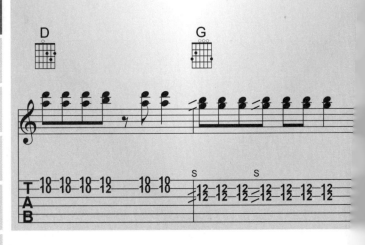

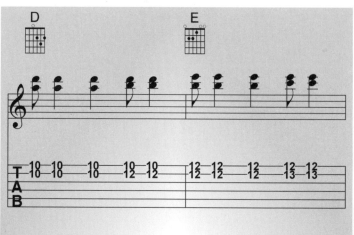

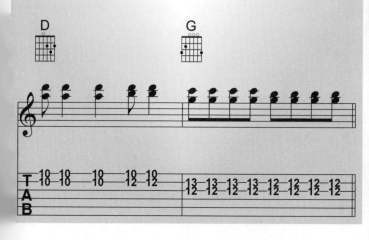

Blues Rock

Hard Rock

Glam Rock

Heavy Metal

Arena Rock

AOR Rock

Punk Rock

Grunge Rock

Indie Rock

Brit pop

Nu Metal

Garage Rock

Example 10 Lead

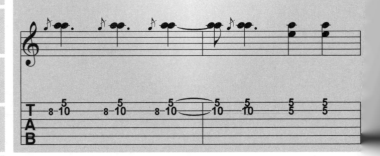

Punk Rock

Blues Rock

Hard Rock

Glam Rock

Heavy Metal

Arena Rock

AOR Rock

Punk Rock

Grunge Rock

Indie Rock

Brit pop

Nu Metal

Garage Rock

Example 11 Lead

Blues
Rock

Hard
Rock

Glam
Rock

Heavy
Metal

Arena
Rock

AOR
Rock

Punk
Rock

Grunge
Rock

Indie
Rock

Brit
pop

Nu
Metal

Garage
Rock

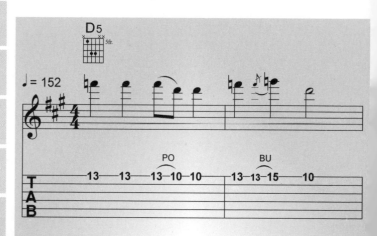

Blues
Rock

Hard
Rock

Glam
Rock

Heavy
Metal

Arena
Rock

AOR
Rock

Punk
Rock

Grunge
Rock

Indie
Rock

Brit
pop

Nu
Metal

Garage
Rock

Example 12 Lead

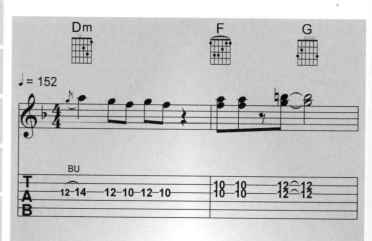

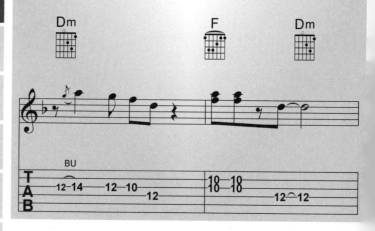

Punk Rock

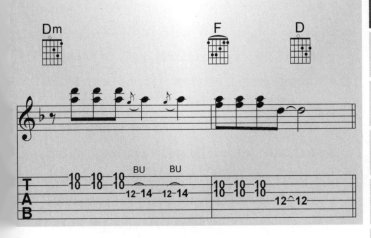

Blues Rock

Hard Rock

Glam Rock

Heavy Metal

Arena Rock

AOR Rock

Punk Rock

Grunge Rock

Indie Rock

Brit pop

Nu Metal

Garage Rock

Blues
Rock

Hard
Rock

Glam
Rock

Heavy
Metal

Arena
Rock

AOR
Rock

Punk
Rock

Grunge
Rock

Indie
Rock

Brit
pop

Nu
Metal

Garage
Rock

Grunge Rock

As the Eighties turned into the Nineties, a rush of loud, raw music emanated from across the northwest of the USA, bands like the Pixies and the Red Hot Chili Peppers ushering in the 'grunge' era. Nirvana guitarist and songwriter, Kurt Cobain, penned songs that combined urgency and noise with incredibly catchy melodies – some even reminiscent of the Beatles. He believed in 'playing whatever you want as sloppy as you want as long as it's good and has passion'.

Grunge guitar, like punk, is based on rhythm guitar patterns with the occasional one- or two-note interjection – think of 'Nevermind's distinctive intro played over a thrumming bass. A distortion pedal definitely helps, especially if like Cobain you favour an entry-level Fender-style guitar with single pickup. You won't get the appropriate 'welly' otherwise. Alternate and down tunings were also in vogue. But the most important thing, and something that can't be taught, was attitude.

Blues
Rock

Hard
Rock

Glam
Rock

Heavy
Metal

Arena
Rock

AOR
Rock

Punk
Rock

Grunge
Rock

Indie
Rock

Brit
pop

Nu
Metal

Garage
Rock

Example 01 Rhythm

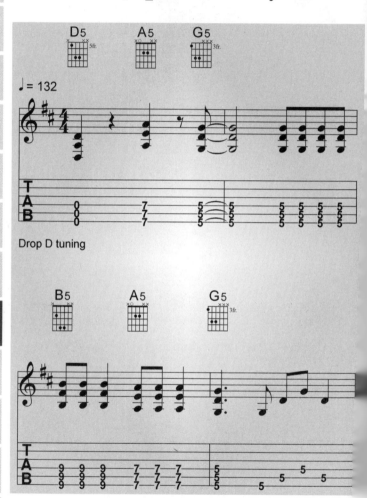

Drop D tuning

Blues Rock

Hard Rock

Garage Rock

Heavy Metal

Arena Rock

AOR Rock

Punk Rock

Grunge Rock

Indie Rock

Brit pop

Nu Metal

Garage Rock

Grunge Rock

Blues Rock

Hard Rock

Glam Rock

Heavy Metal

Arena Rock

AOR Rock

Punk Rock

Grunge Rock

Indie Rock

Brit pop

Nu Metal

Garage Rock

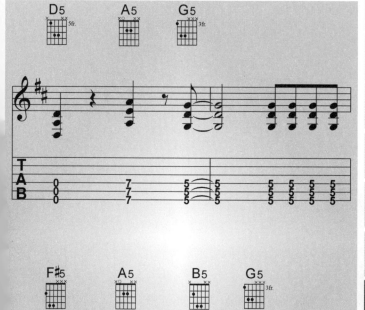

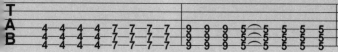

241

Example 02 Rhythm

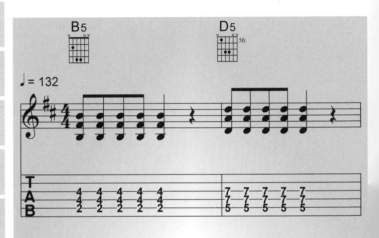

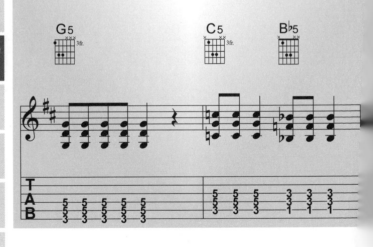

Grunge Rock

Blues Rock

Hard Rock

Glam Rock

Heavy Metal

Arena Rock

AOR Rock

Punk Rock

Grunge Rock

Indie Rock

Brit pop

Nu Metal

Garage Rock

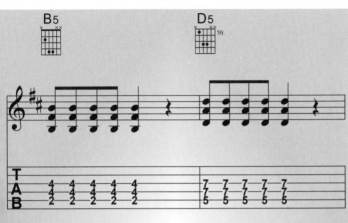

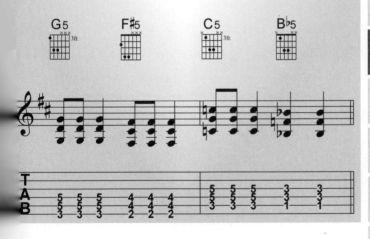

243

Example 03 Rhythm

Blues Rock

Hard Rock

Garage Rock

Heavy Metal

Arena Rock

AOR Rock

Punk Rock

Grunge Rock

Indie Rock

Brit pop

Nu Metal

Garage Rock

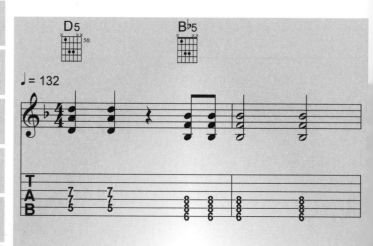

244

Grunge Rock

Blues
Rock

Hard
Rock

Glam
Rock

Heavy
Metal

Arena
Rock

AOR
Rock

Punk
Rock

Grunge
Rock

Indie
Rock

Brit
pop

Nu
Metal

Garage
Rock

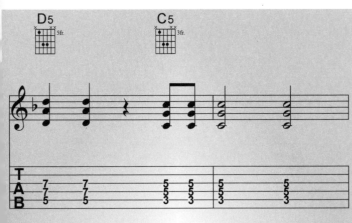

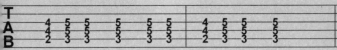

Example 04 Rhythm

Blues
Rock

Hard
Rock

Glam
Rock

Heavy
Metal

Arena
Rock

AOR
Rock

Punk
Rock

Grunge
Rock

Indie
Rock

Brit
pop

Nu
Metal

Garage
Rock

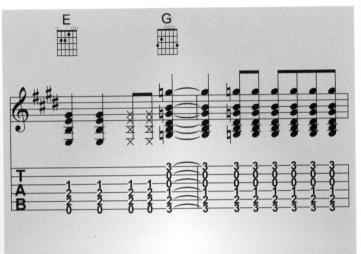

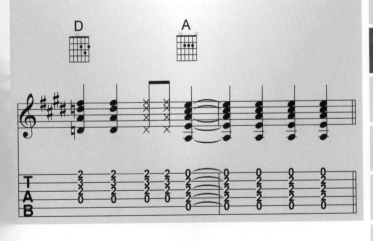

Example 05 Riff

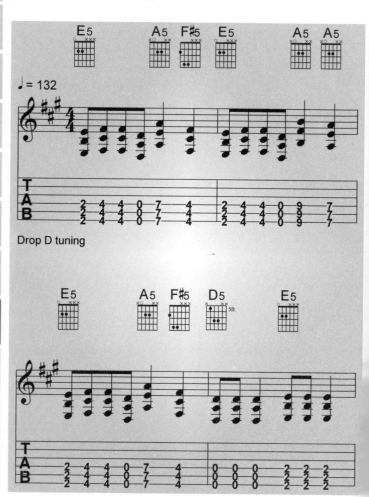

Drop D tuning

Grunge Rock

Blues
Rock

Hard
Rock

Glam
Rock

Heavy
Metal

Arena
Rock

AOR
Rock

Punk
Rock

Grunge
Rock

Indie
Rock

Brit
pop

Nu
Metal

Garage
Rock

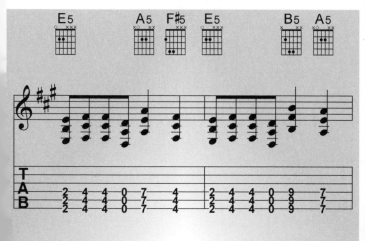

249

Example 06 Riff

Blues Rock

Hard Rock

Garage Rock

Heavy Metal

Arena Rock

AOR Rock

Punk Rock

Grunge Rock

Indie Rock

Brit pop

Nu Metal

Garage Rock

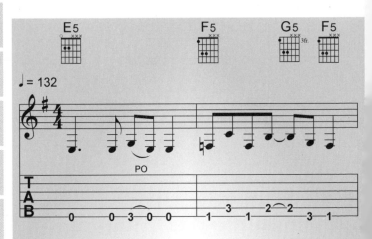

Grunge Rock

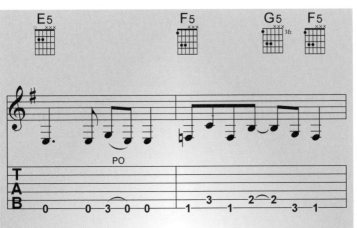

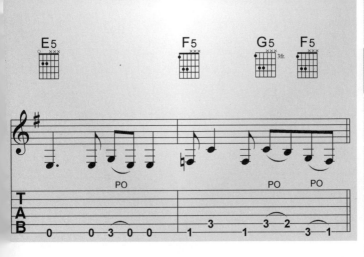

Blues Rock

Hard Rock

Glam Rock

Heavy Metal

Arena Rock

AOR Rock

Punk Rock

Grunge Rock

Indie Rock

Brit pop

Nu Metal

Garage Rock

Example 07 Riff

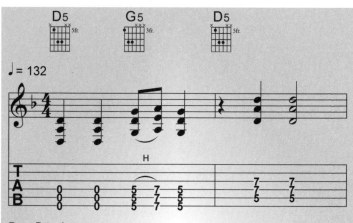

Drop D tuning

Grunge Rock

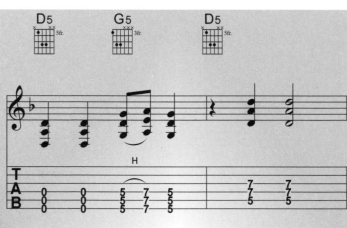

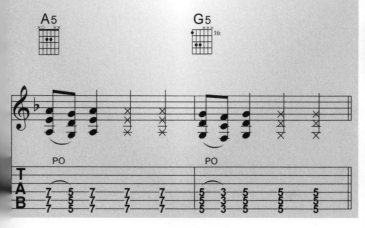

Blues Rock

Hard Rock

Glam Rock

Heavy Metal

Arena Rock

AOR Rock

Punk Rock

Grunge Rock

Indie Rock

Brit pop

Nu Metal

Garage Rock

Example 08 Riff

Grunge Rock

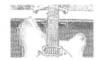

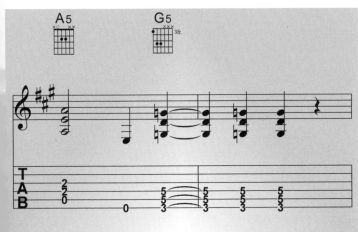

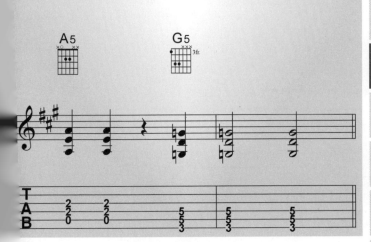

Blues Rock

Hard Rock

Glam Rock

Heavy Metal

Arena Rock

AOR Rock

Punk Rock

Grunge Rock

Indie Rock

Brit pop

Nu Metal

Garage Rock

Example 09 Lead

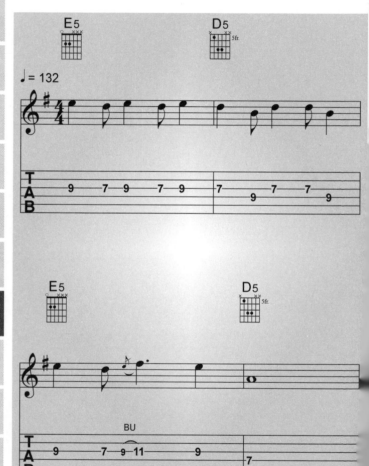

Grunge Rock

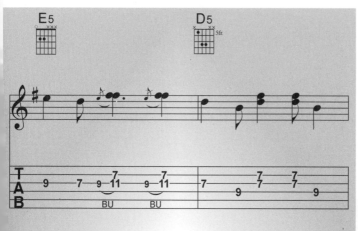

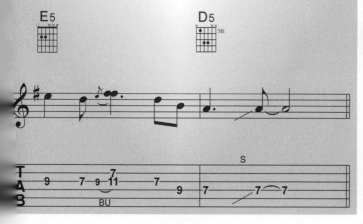

Blues Rock

Hard Rock

Glam Rock

Heavy Metal

Arena Rock

AOR Rock

Punk Rock

Grunge Rock

Indie Rock

Brit pop

Nu Metal

Garage Rock

Example 10 Lead

Blues Rock

Hard Rock

Garage Rock

Heavy Metal

Arena Rock

AOR Rock

Punk Rock

Grunge Rock

Indie Rock

Brit pop

Nu Metal

Garage Rock

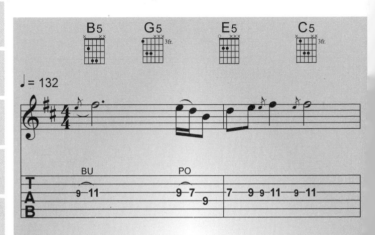

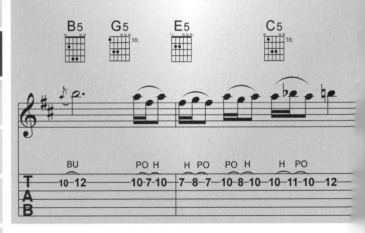

Grunge Rock

Blues Rock

Hard Rock

Glam Rock

Heavy Metal

Arena Rock

AOR Rock

Punk Rock

Grunge Rock

Indie Rock

Brit pop

Nu Metal

Garage Rock

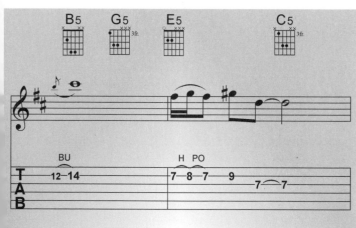

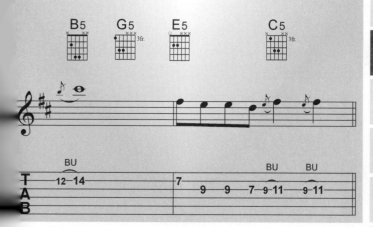

Example 11 Lead

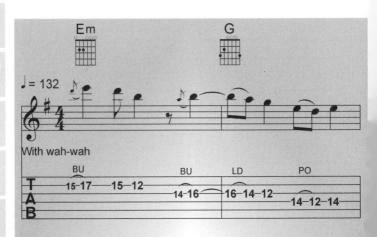

With wah-wah

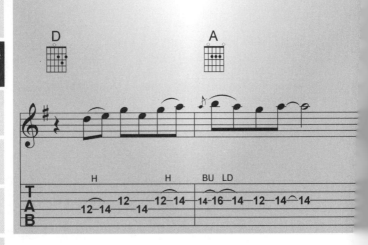

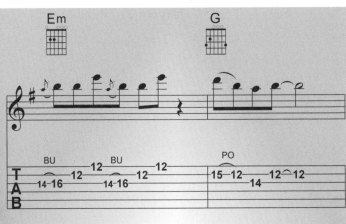

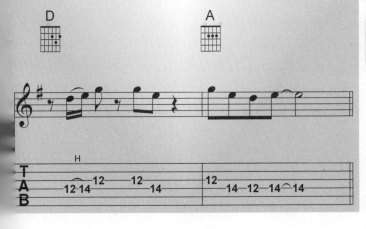

Blues Rock

Hard Rock

Glam Rock

Heavy Metal

Arena Rock

AOR Rock

Punk Rock

Grunge Rock

Indie Rock

Brit pop

Nu Metal

Garage Rock

Example 12 Lead

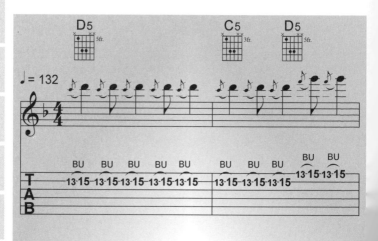

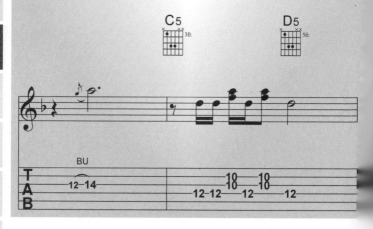

Grunge Rock

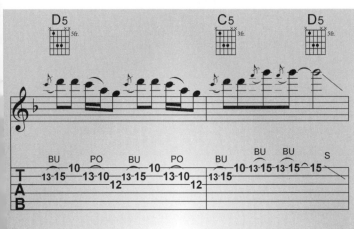

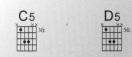

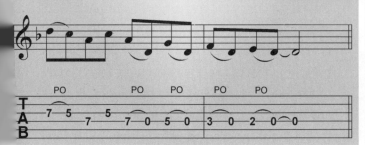

Blues Rock

Hard Rock

Glam Rock

Heavy Metal

Arena Rock

AOR Rock

Punk Rock

Grunge Rock

Indie Rock

Brit pop

Nu Metal

Garage Rock

Blues
Rock

Hard
Rock

Glam
Rock

Heavy
Metal

Arena
Rock

AOR
Rock

Punk
Rock

Grunge
Rock

Indie
Rock

Brit
pop

Nu
Metal

Garage
Rock

Indie Rock

The guitar styles of indie rock can vary from the jaunty arpeggios of Johnny Marr's Rickenbacker that propelled the Smiths to stardom, to the sheets of sound Radiohead guitarists Ed O'Brien and Jonny Greenwood conjure up. Marr's main influence was folk rock and his appreciation of melody and structure meant that he was later employed by Paul McCartney, Chrissie Hynde and others, and was the main influence on the aforementioned Radiohead players.

As they developed, O'Brien and Greenwood mixed in a German influence from Can and, from nearer home, recognized the genius of John McGeoch. Formerly with Magazine, McGeoch also played with Siouxsie and the Banshees, preferring to add texture and shade to songs rather than all-out soloing. Coldplay and Muse also took a leaf out of Radiohead's book, arguably basing their sound on 2000's chart-topping Kid A album, while Stereophonics' Kelly Jones and the Manic Street Preachers' James Dean Bradfield took a Welsh perspective with Gibson guitars and fractured chords a-plenty.

Blues
Rock

Hard
Rock

Glam
Rock

Heavy
Metal

Arena
Rock

AOR
Rock

Punk
Rock

Grunge
Rock

**Indie
Rock**

Brit
pop

Nu
Metal

Garage
Rock

Example 01 Rhythm

Blues Rock

Hard Rock

Glam Rock

Heavy Metal

Arena Rock

AOR Rock

Punk Rock

Grunge Rock

Indie Rock

Brit pop

Nu Metal

Garage Rock

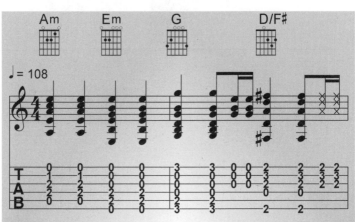

Jangly clean sound

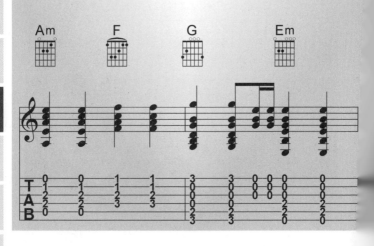

Indie Rock

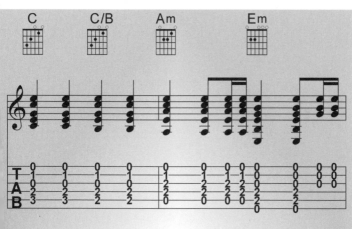

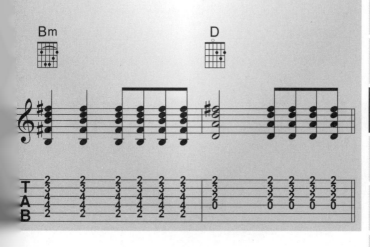

Blues Rock

Hard Rock

Glam Rock

Heavy Metal

Arena Rock

AOR Rock

Punk Rock

Grunge Rock

Indie Rock

Brit pop

Nu Metal

Garage Rock

Example 02 Rhythm

Blues
Rock

Hard
Rock

Glam
Rock

Heavy
Metal

Arena
Rock

AOR
Rock

Punk
Rock

Grunge
Rock

**Indie
Rock**

Brit
pop

Nu
Metal

Garage
Rock

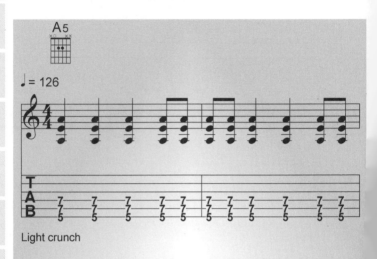

Light crunch

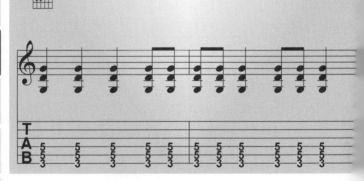

Indie Rock

Blues Rock

Hard Rock

Glam Rock

Heavy Metal

Arena Rock

AOR Rock

Punk Rock

Grunge Rock

Indie Rock

Brit pop

Nu Metal

Garage Rock

E5

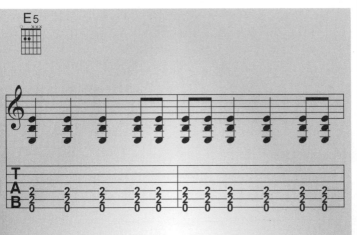

B5

Example 03 Rhythm

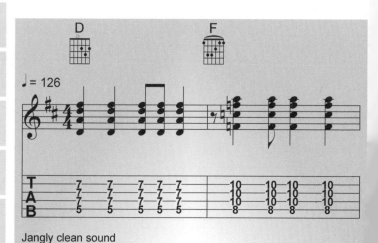

Jangly clean sound

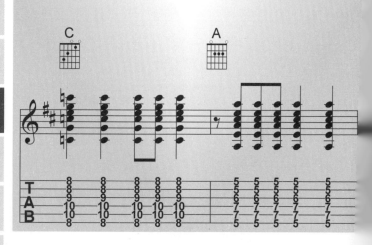

Indie Rock

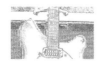

Blues Rock

Hard Rock

Glam Rock

Heavy Metal

Arena Rock

AOR Rock

Punk Rock

Grunge Rock

Indie Rock

Brit pop

Nu Metal

Garage Rock

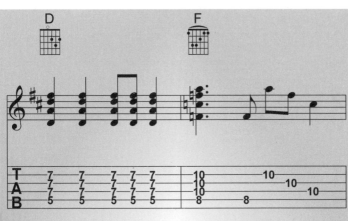

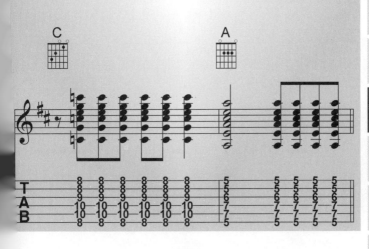

271

Example 04 Rhythm

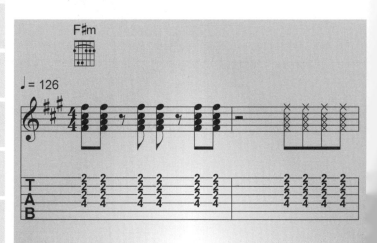

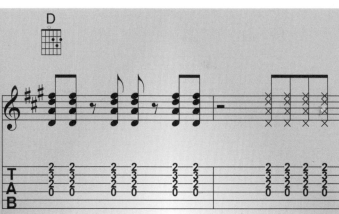

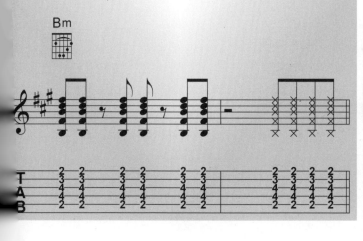

Blues Rock

Hard Rock

Glam Rock

Heavy Metal

Arena Rock

AOR Rock

Punk Rock

Grunge Rock

Indie Rock

Brit pop

Nu Metal

Garage Rock

Example 05 Riff

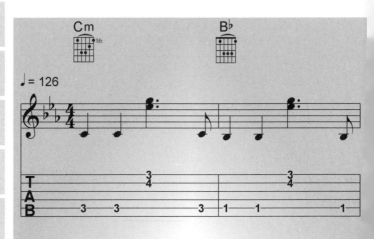

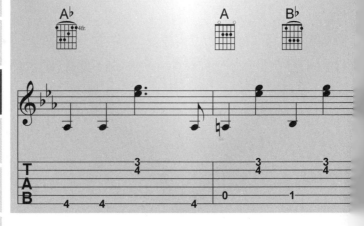

274

Indie Rock

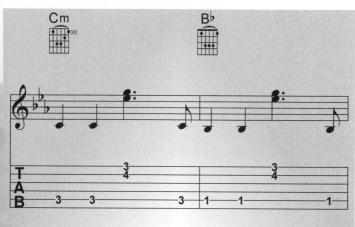

Blues Rock

Hard Rock

Glam Rock

Heavy Metal

Arena Rock

AOR Rock

Punk Rock

Grunge Rock

Indie Rock

Brit pop

Nu Metal

Garage Rock

Example 06 Riff

A5 C5 G5 B5

♩ = 126

A5 C5 G5 F#5 F5

276

Indie Rock

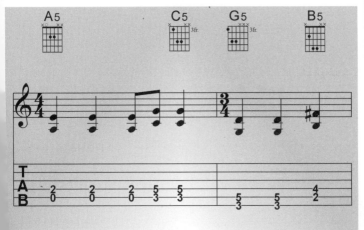

Blues Rock

Hard Rock

Glam Rock

Heavy Metal

Arena Rock

AOR Rock

Punk Rock

Grunge Rock

Indie Rock

Brit pop

Nu Metal

Garage Rock

Example 07 Riff

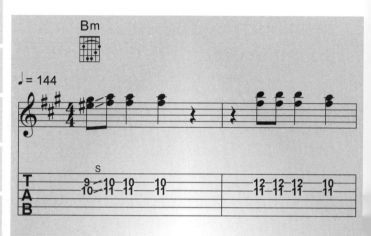

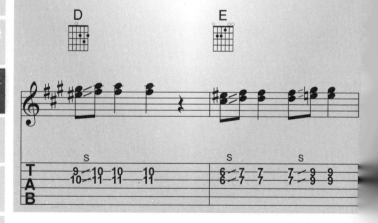

Indie Rock

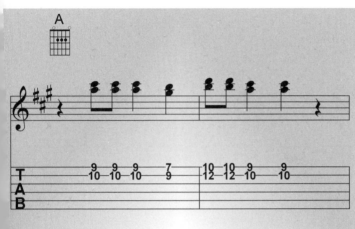

Blues Rock

Hard Rock

Glam Rock

Heavy Metal

Arena Rock

AOR Rock

Punk Rock

Grunge Rock

Indie Rock

Brit pop

Nu Metal

Garage Rock

Example 08 Riff

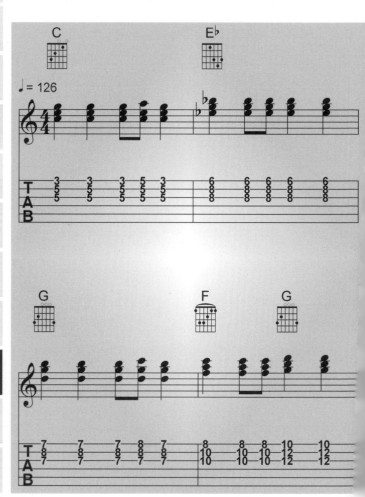

Indie Rock

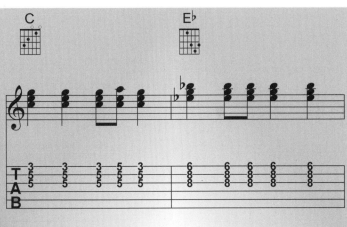

Blues Rock

Hard Rock

Glam Rock

Heavy Metal

Arena Rock

AOR Rock

Punk Rock

Grunge Rock

Indie Rock

Brit pop

Nu Metal

Garage Rock

Example 09 Lead

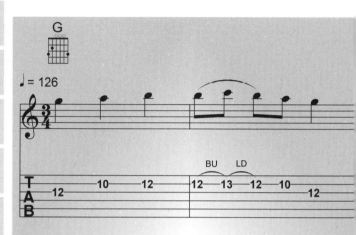

Blues Rock

Hard Rock

Glam Rock

Heavy Metal

Arena Rock

AOR Rock

Punk Rock

Grunge Rock

Indie Rock

Brit pop

Nu Metal

Garage Rock

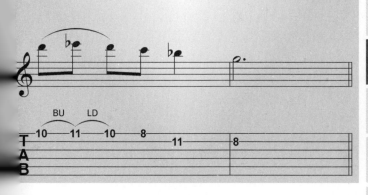

Example 10 Lead

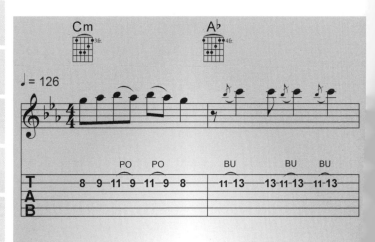

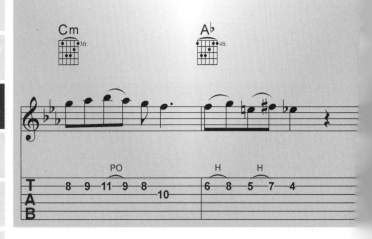

Indie Rock

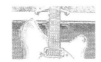

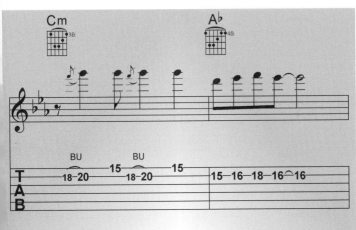

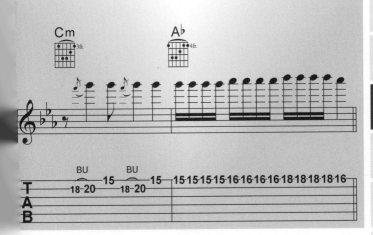

Blues Rock

Hard Rock

Glam Rock

Heavy Metal

Arena Rock

AOR Rock

Punk Rock

Grunge Rock

Indie Rock

Brit pop

Nu Metal

Garage Rock

Example 11 Lead

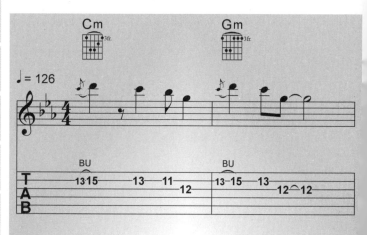

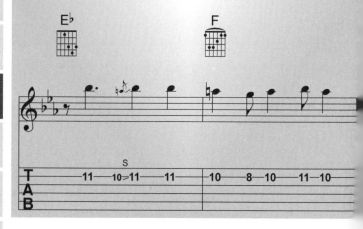

Indie Rock

Blues Rock

Hard Rock

Glam Rock

Heavy Metal

Arena Rock

AOR Rock

Punk Rock

Grunge Rock

Indie Rock

Brit pop

Nu Metal

Garage Rock

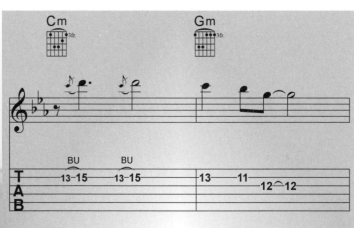

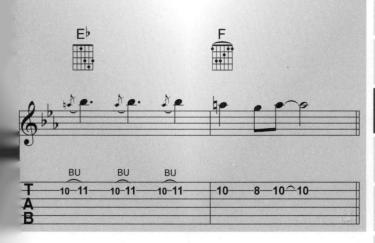

Example 12 Lead

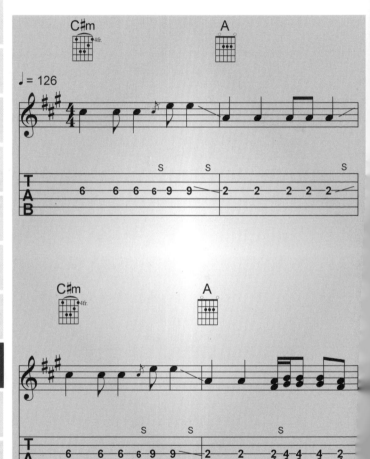

Indie Rock

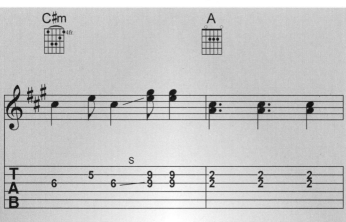

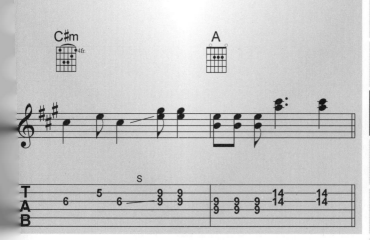

Blues Rock

Hard Rock

Glam Rock

Heavy Metal

Arena Rock

AOR Rock

Punk Rock

Grunge Rock

Indie Rock

Brit pop

Nu Metal

Garage Rock

Blues
Rock

Hard
Rock

Glam
Rock

Heavy
Metal

Arena
Rock

AOR
Rock

Punk
Rock

Grunge
Rock

Indie
Rock

Brit
pop

Nu
Metal

Garage
Rock

Britpop

The guitarists who played the biggest part in Britpop, Noel Gallagher and Graham Coxon, took a time machine back 30 years to the mid-Sixties and the chiming styles of the Beatles, Kinks and Stones. Playing classic instruments like the Epiphone Casino semi-acoustic, Gallagher's emphasis was on creating classic melodies. Progressions running through major sevenths and sevenths were favourites.

The La's, Pulp, Teenage Fanclub and Embrace were among the groups who used simple open chords and fingerpicking to evoke an atmosphere. Paul Weller, the godfather of Britpop, had a penchant for open minor chords, while John Squire of the Stone Roses favoured big, full-sounding barre chords. While Britpop tended to play to the 'rules' and broke few boundaries, it wasn't so much what was used as the way it was used. Note must also be made of the work of Bernard Butler, guitarist with Suede, who took inspiration from folk and blues to create exquisite riffs and inspire many players of the future.

Blues
Rock

Hard
Rock

Glam
Rock

Heavy
Metal

Arena
Rock

AOR
Rock

Punk
Rock

Grunge
Rock

Indie
Rock

**Brit
pop**

Nu
Metal

Garage
Rock

Example 01 Rhythm

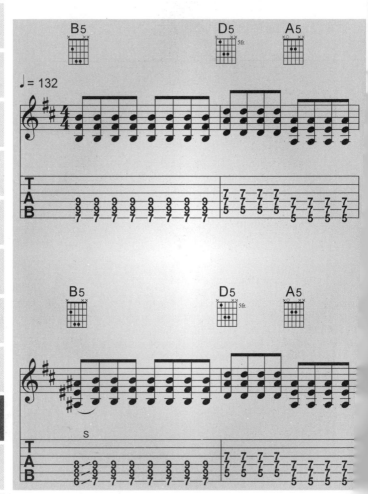

Britpop

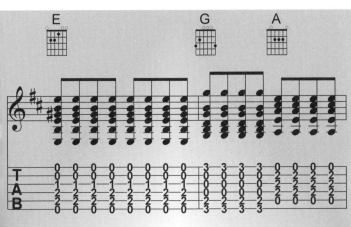

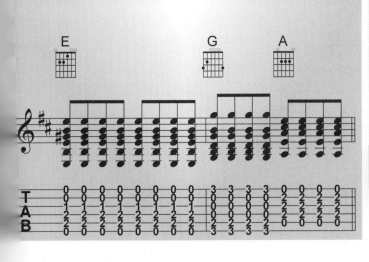

Example 02 Rhythm

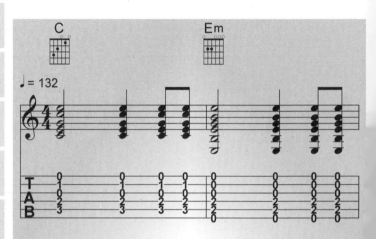

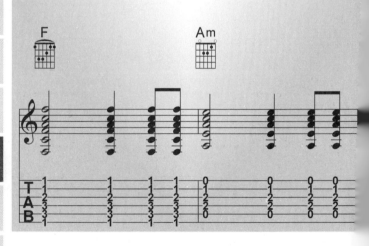

Britpop

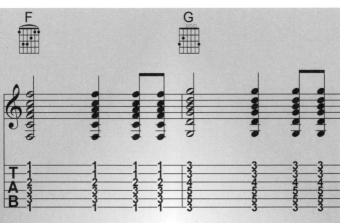

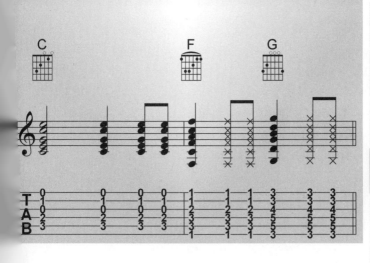

Blues Rock

Hard Rock

Glam Rock

Heavy Metal

Arena Rock

AOR Rock

Punk Rock

Grunge Rock

Indie Rock

Brit pop

Nu Metal

Garage Rock

Example 03 Rhythm

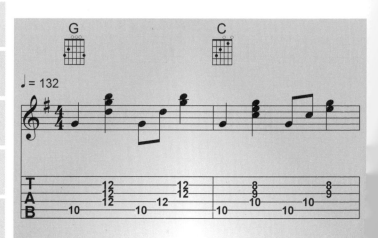

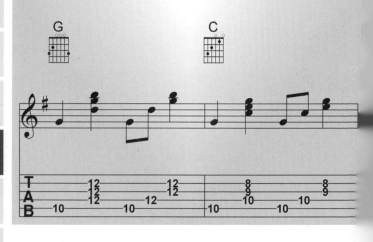

Britpop

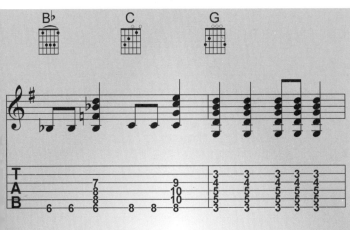

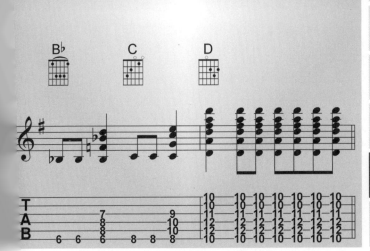

Blues Rock

Hard Rock

Glam Rock

Heavy Metal

Arena Rock

AOR Rock

Punk Rock

Grunge Rock

Indie Rock

Brit pop

Nu Metal

Garage Rock

Example 04 Rhythm

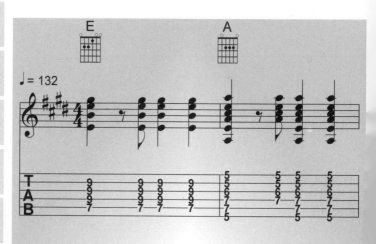

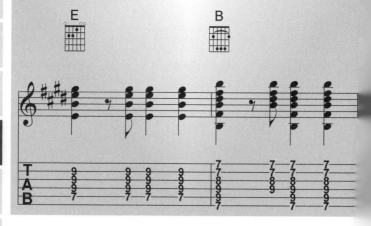

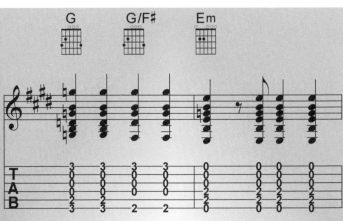

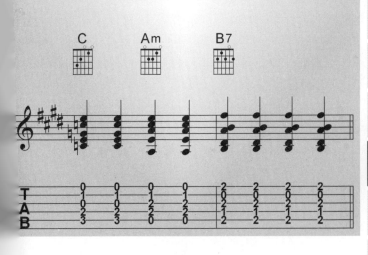

Blues Rock

Hard Rock

Glam Rock

Heavy Metal

Arena Rock

AOR Rock

Punk Rock

Grunge Rock

Indie Rock

Brit pop

Nu Metal

Garage Rock

Example 05 Riff

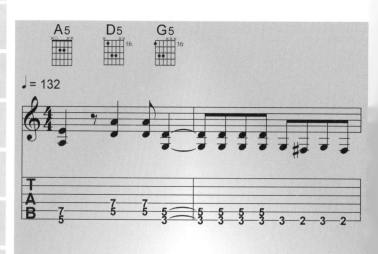

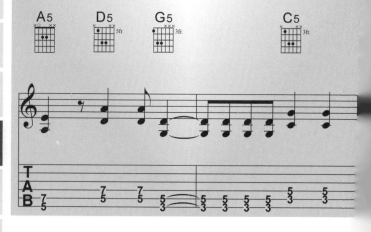

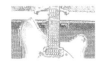

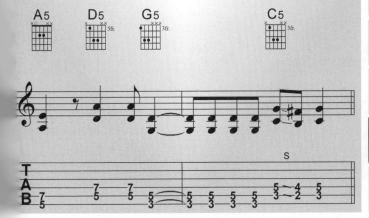

Blues Rock

Hard Rock

Glam Rock

Heavy Metal

Arena Rock

AOR Rock

Punk Rock

Grunge Rock

Indie Rock

Brit pop

Nu Metal

Garage Rock

Example 06 Riff

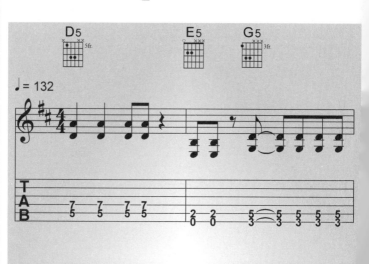

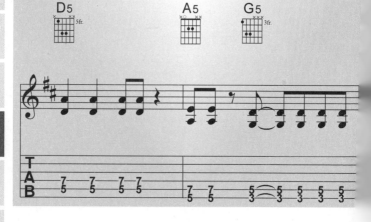

Britpop

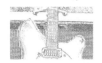

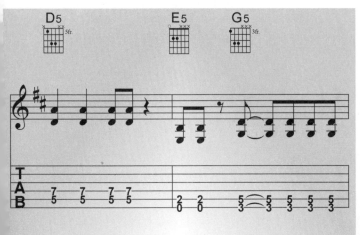

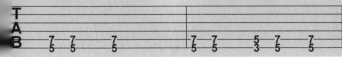

Blues Rock

Hard Rock

Glam Rock

Heavy Metal

Arena Rock

AOR Rock

Punk Rock

Grunge Rock

Indie Rock

Brit pop

Nu Metal

Garage Rock

Example 07 Riff

Blues Rock

Hard Rock

Glam Rock

Heavy Metal

Arena Rock

AOR Rock

Punk Rock

Grunge Rock

Indie Rock

Brit pop

Nu Metal

Garage Rock

Britpop

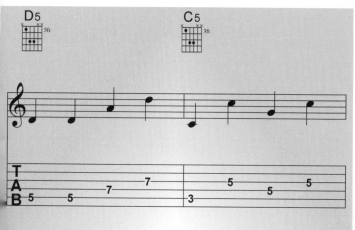

Blues Rock

Hard Rock

Glam Rock

Heavy Metal

Arena Rock

AOR Rock

Punk Rock

Grunge Rock

Indie Rock

Brit pop

Nu Metal

Garage Rock

Example 08 Riff

Britpop

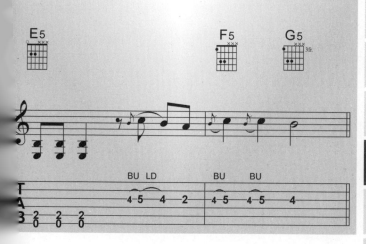

Blues Rock

Hard Rock

Glam Rock

Heavy Metal

Arena Rock

AOR Rock

Punk Rock

Grunge Rock

Indie Rock

Brit pop

Nu Metal

Garage Rock

Example 09 Lead

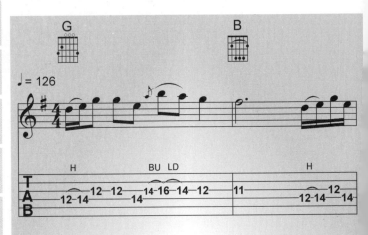

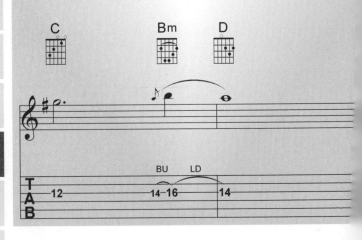

Britpop

Blues Rock

Hard Rock

Glam Rock

Heavy Metal

Arena Rock

AOR Rock

Punk Rock

Grunge Rock

Indie Rock

Brit pop

Nu Metal

Garage Rock

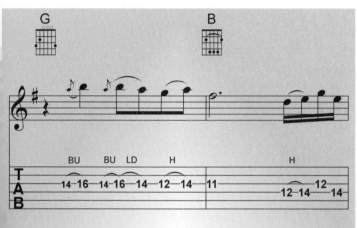

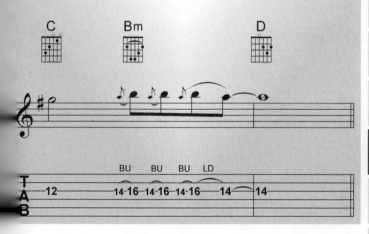

309

Example 10 Lead

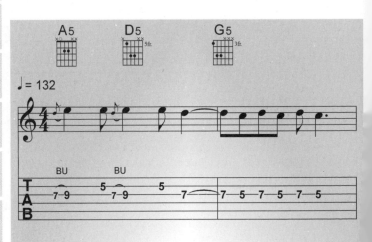

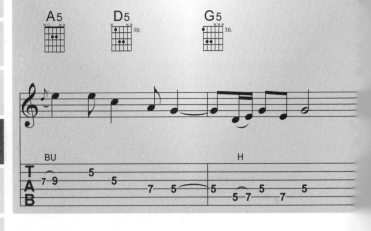

Britpop

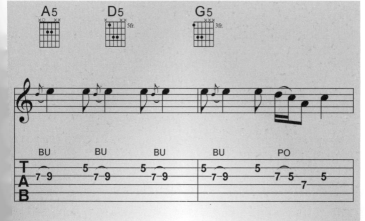

Blues Rock

Hard Rock

Glam Rock

Heavy Metal

Arena Rock

AOR Rock

Punk Rock

Grunge Rock

Indie Rock

Brit pop

Nu Metal

Garage Rock

Example 11 Lead

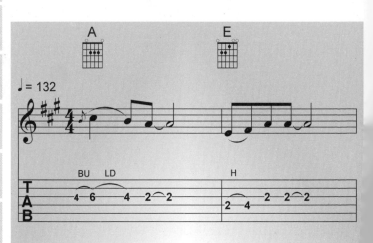

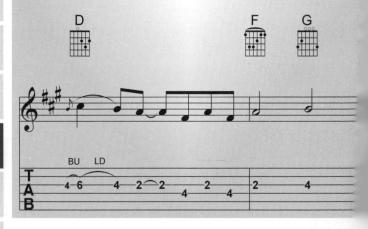

Britpop

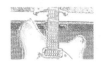

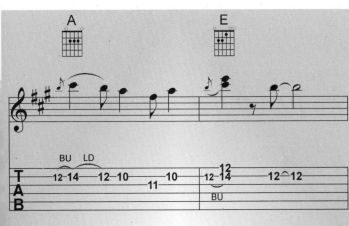

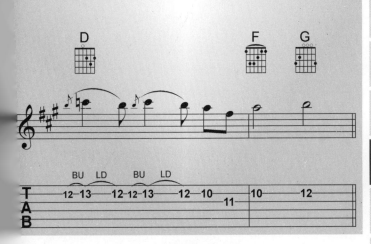

Blues Rock

Hard Rock

Glam Rock

Heavy Metal

Arena Rock

AOR Rock

Punk Rock

Grunge Rock

Indie Rock

Brit pop

Nu Metal

Garage Rock

Example 12 Lead

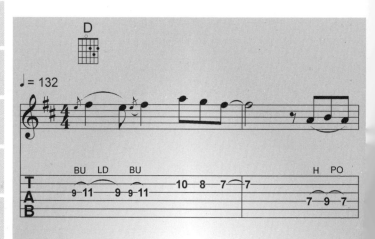

Blues Rock
Hard Rock
Glam Rock
Heavy Metal
Arena Rock
AOR Rock
Punk Rock
Grunge Rock
Indie Rock
Brit pop
Nu Metal
Garage Rock

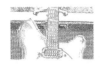

Blues Rock

Hard Rock

Glam Rock

Heavy Metal

Arena Rock

AOR Rock

Punk Rock

Grunge Rock

Indie Rock

Brit pop

Nu Metal

Garage Rock

Blues
Rock

Hard
Rock

Glam
Rock

Heavy
Metal

Arena
Rock

AOR
Rock

Punk
Rock

Grunge
Rock

Indie
Rock

Brit
pop

Nu
Metal

Garage
Rock

Nu Metal

The terms 'nu metal' and 'nu rock' are used to describe bands like Korn, Limp Bizkit, Slipknot, the Deftones, Amen and Papa Roach who appeared in the decade following Nirvana's all-conquering popularity in the early Nineties – post grunge is another label often used. The music often incorporated characteristics of grunge, like distorted guitar, angst-filled lyrics and the dynamics (loud chorus contrasting with quiet verse), but reproduced it in a more radio-friendly, commercial way. This ensured the genre's mainstream popularity, but arguably gave it excessive exposure that caused an inevitable backlash.

Guitar was only part of the formula, and, as with grunge, solos were few and far between. The emphasis was on texture rather than melody, with rhythmic, distorted riffs often played on detuned strings with palm muting to create a dark, threatening sound. But as Limp Bizkit found when they lost Wes Borland, it was an important part indeed. Borland had used seven-string and four-string Ibanez guitars to achieve his desired effect.

Blues
Rock

Hard
Rock

Glam
Rock

Heavy
Metal

Arena
Rock

AOR
Rock

Punk
Rock

Grunge
Rock

Indie
Rock

Brit
pop

**Nu
Metal**

Garage
Rock

Example 01 Rhythm

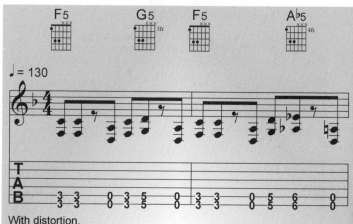

With distortion.
6th string to D.

Nu Metal

Blues Rock

Hard Rock

Glam Rock

Heavy Metal

Arena Rock

AOR Rock

Punk Rock

Grunge Rock

Indie Rock

Brit pop

Nu Metal

Garage Rock

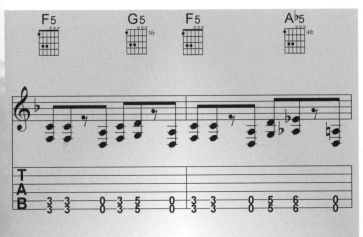

Example 02 Rhythm

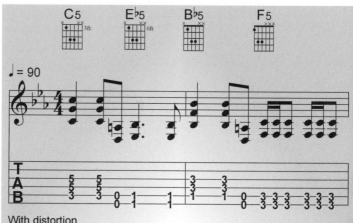

With distortion.
6th string to D.

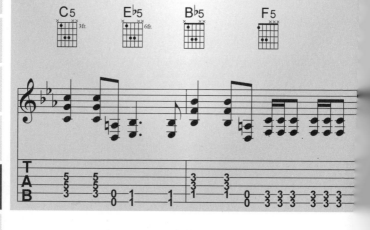

Nu Metal

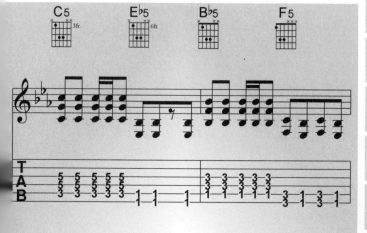

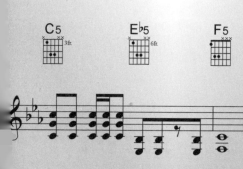

Example 03 Rhythm

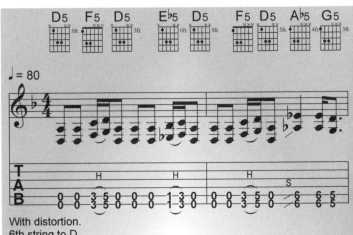

With distortion.
6th string to D.

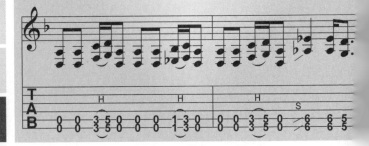

Nu Metal

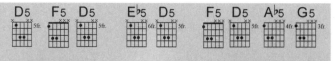

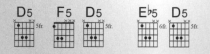

Blues Rock

Hard Rock

Glam Rock

Heavy Metal

Arena Rock

AOR Rock

Punk Rock

Grunge Rock

Indie Rock

Brit pop

Nu Metal

Garage Rock

323

Example 04 Rhythm

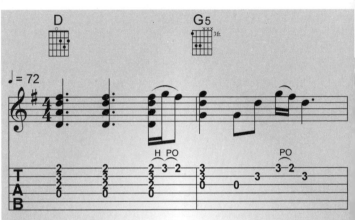

With clean sound.

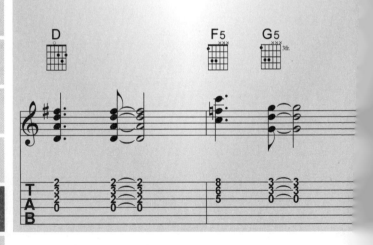

Blues Rock

Hard Rock

Glam Rock

Heavy Metal

Arena Rock

AOR Rock

Punk Rock

Grunge Rock

Indie Rock

Brit pop

Nu Metal

Garage Rock

Nu Metal

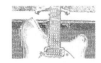

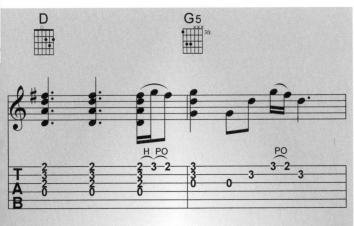

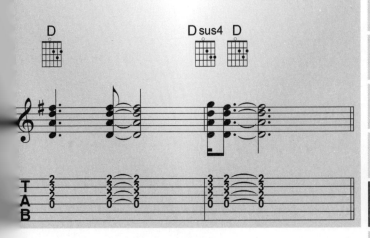

Blues
Rock

Hard
Rock

Glam
Rock

Heavy
Metal

Arena
Rock

AOR
Rock

Punk
Rock

Grunge
Rock

Indie
Rock

Brit
pop

Nu
Metal

Garage
Rock

Example 05 Rhythm

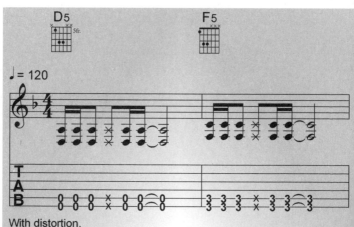

With distortion.
6th string to D.

Nu Metal

Blues Rock

Hard Rock

Glam Rock

Heavy Metal

Arena Rock

AOR Rock

Punk Rock

Grunge Rock

Indie Rock

Brit pop

Nu Metal

Garage Rock

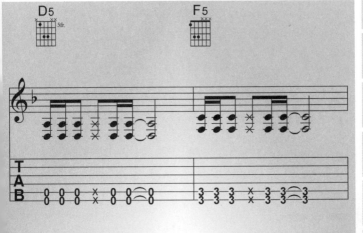

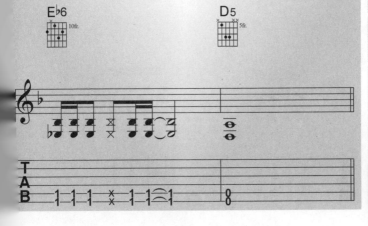

Example 06 Riff

Blues
Rock

Hard
Rock

Glam
Rock

Heavy
Metal

Arena
Rock

AOR
Rock

Punk
Rock

Grunge
Rock

Indie
Rock

Brit
pop

Nu
Metal

Garage
Rock

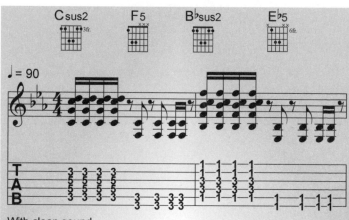

With clean sound.
6th string to D.

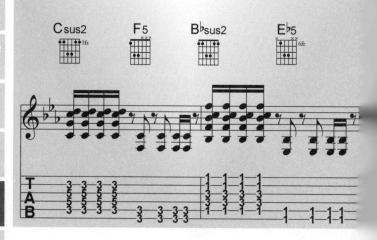

Nu Metal

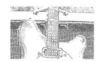

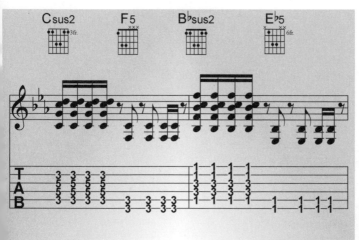

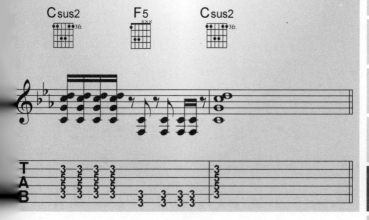

Blues Rock

Hard Rock

Glam Rock

Heavy Metal

Arena Rock

AOR Rock

Punk Rock

Grunge Rock

Indie Rock

Brit pop

Nu Metal

Garage Rock

Example 07 Riff

Blues
Rock

Hard
Rock

Glam
Rock

Heavy
Metal

Arena
Rock

AOR
Rock

Punk
Rock

Grunge
Rock

Indie
Rock

Brit
pop

Nu
Metal

Garage
Rock

With distortion.
6th string to D.

Nu Metal

Blues Rock

Hard Rock

Glam Rock

Heavy Metal

Arena Rock

AOR Rock

Punk Rock

Grunge Rock

Indie Rock

Brit pop

Nu Metal

Garage Rock

Example 08 Riff

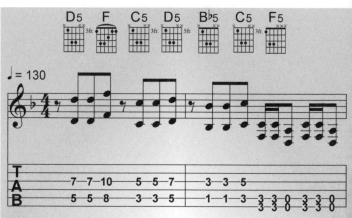

With distortion.
6th string to D.

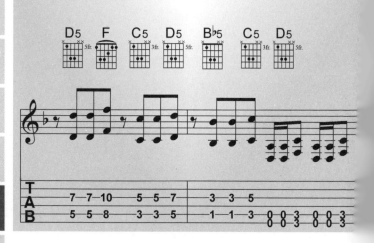

Nu Metal

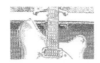

Blues Rock

Hard Rock

Glam Rock

Heavy Metal

Arena Rock

AOR Rock

Punk Rock

Grunge Rock

Indie Rock

Brit pop

Nu Metal

Garage Rock

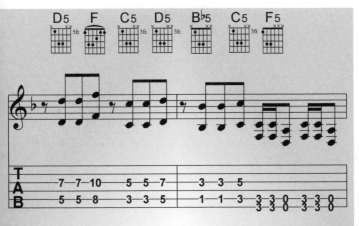

Example 09 Riff

Blues Rock

Hard Rock

Glam Rock

Heavy Metal

Arena Rock

AOR Rock

Punk Rock

Grunge Rock

Indie Rock

Brit pop

Nu Metal

Garage Rock

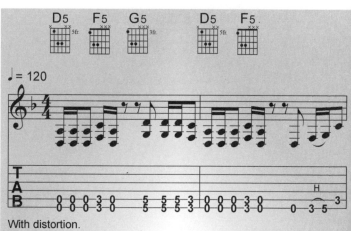

With distortion.
6th string to D.

Nu Metal

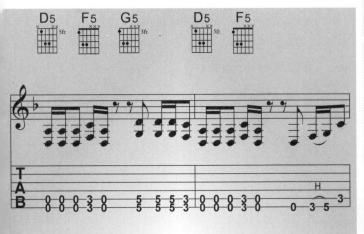

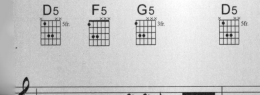

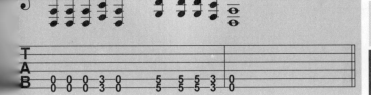

Blues Rock

Hard Rock

Glam Rock

Heavy Metal

Arena Rock

AOR Rock

Punk Rock

Grunge Rock

Indie Rock

Brit pop

Nu Metal

Garage Rock

Blues Rock

Hard Rock

Glam Rock

Heavy Metal

Arena Rock

AOR Rock

Punk Rock

Grunge Rock

Indie Rock

Brit pop

Nu Metal

Garage Rock

Example 10 Lead

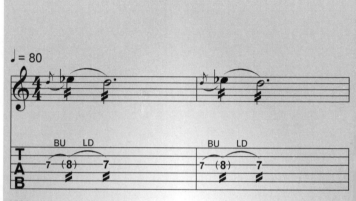

With echo and distortion.

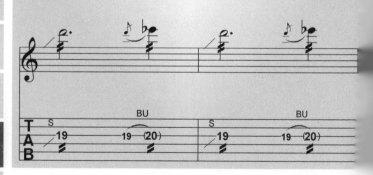

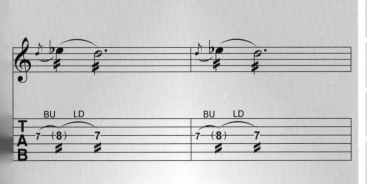

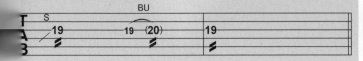

Blues Rock

Hard Rock

Glam Rock

Heavy Metal

Arena Rock

AOR Rock

Punk Rock

Grunge Rock

Indie Rock

Brit pop

Nu Metal

Garage Rock

Example 11 Lead

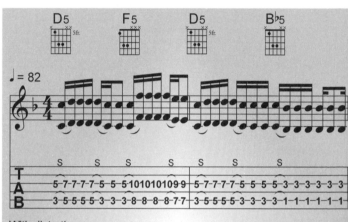

With distortion.

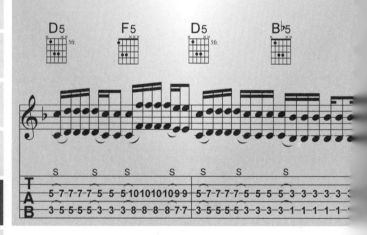

Nu Metal

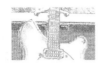

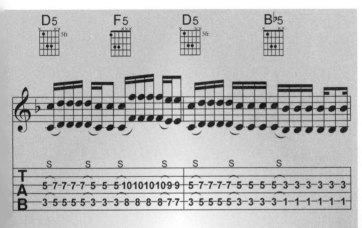

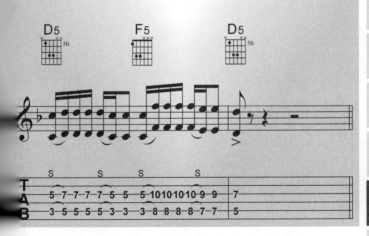

Blues Rock

Hard Rock

Glam Rock

Heavy Metal

Arena Rock

AOR Rock

Punk Rock

Grunge Rock

Indie Rock

Brit pop

Nu Metal

Garage Rock

Example 12 Lead

Blues Rock

Hard Rock

Glam Rock

Heavy Metal

Arena Rock

AOR Rock

Punk Rock

Grunge Rock

Indie Rock

Brit pop

Nu Metal

Garage Rock

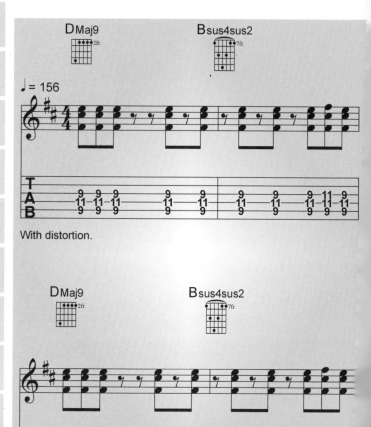

With distortion.

Nu Metal

Blues
Rock

Hard
Rock

Glam
Rock

Heavy
Metal

Arena
Rock

AOR
Rock

Punk
Rock

Grunge
Rock

Indie
Rock

Brit
pop

Nu
Metal

Garage
Rock

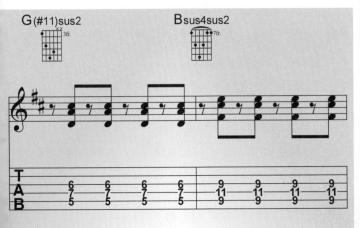

G(#11)sus2   Bsus4sus2

DMaj9   DMaj9

Garage Rock

The Sixties found American youth heading for the garage to create memorable low-fi music in the shape of bands like the Shadows of Knight and the Seeds. That excitement was revisited in the Nineties by the likes of the White Stripes, the Strokes, the Hives and the Vines. Hoarse vocals and hammering drums compete with basic guitar riffs played on retro equipment. Players like Jack White of the White Stripes tended to play most of their songs at the lower end of the neck, often playing basic or fragmentary chords and applying the thumb from over the top of the fretboard to make 'barred' bass chords. Tuning was often rudimentary, while effects like octave dividers, distortions, compression and sustain were all applied.

By colouring outside the lines, garage rock brought back excitement to rock in a punk-like way. Some of the riffs introduced, such as those on the White Stripes' 'Seven Nation Army', will endure for as long as rock is listened to.

Blues
Rock

Hard
Rock

Glam
Rock

Heavy
Metal

Arena
Rock

AOR
Rock

Punk
Rock

Grunge
Rock

Indie
Rock

Brit
pop

Nu
Metal

Garage
Rock

Example 01 Rhythm

Blues
Rock

Hard
Rock

Glam
Rock

Heavy
Metal

Arena
Rock

AOR
Rock

Punk
Rock

Grunge
Rock

Indie
Rock

Brit
pop

Nu
Metal

Garage
Rock

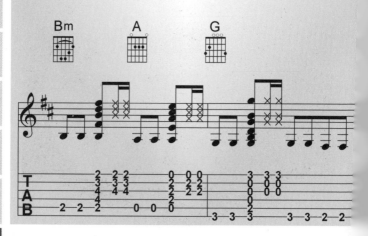

344

Garage Rock

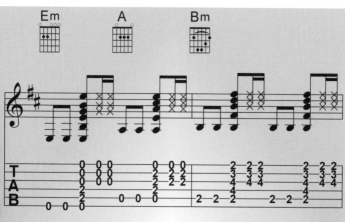

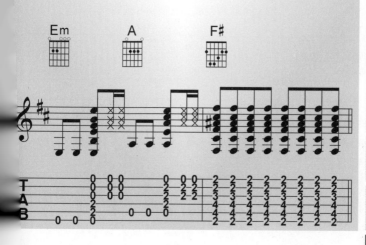

Blues Rock

Hard Rock

Glam Rock

Heavy Metal

Arena Rock

AOR Rock

Punk Rock

Grunge Rock

Indie Rock

Brit pop

Nu Metal

Garage Rock

Example 02 Rhythm

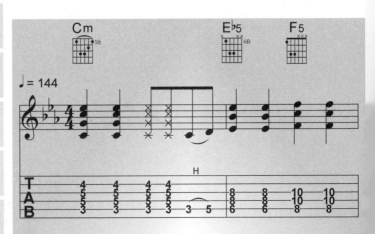

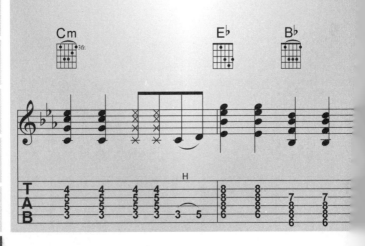

Garage Rock

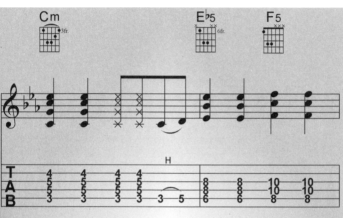

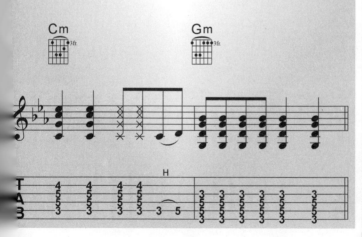

Blues Rock

Hard Rock

Glam Rock

Heavy Metal

Arena Rock

AOR Rock

Punk Rock

Grunge Rock

Indie Rock

Brit pop

Nu Metal

Garage Rock

Example 03 Rhythm

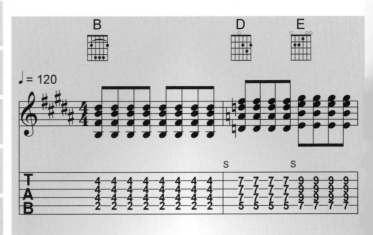

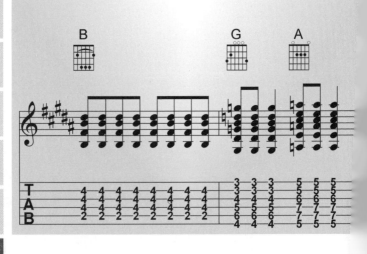

Garage Rock

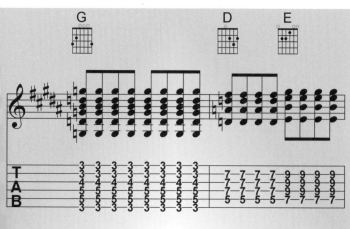

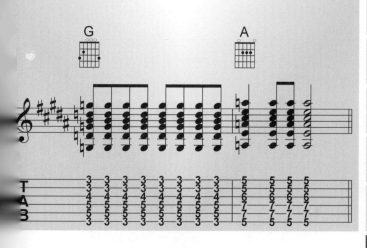

Blues Rock

Hard Rock

Glam Rock

Heavy Metal

Arena Rock

AOR Rock

Punk Rock

Grunge Rock

Indie Rock

Brit pop

Nu Metal

Garage Rock

Example 04 Rhythm

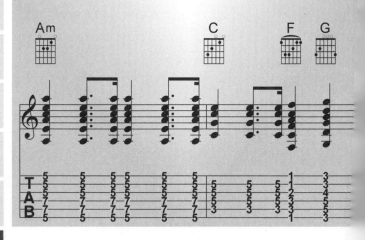

Garage Rock

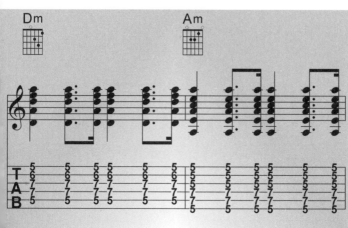

Blues Rock

Hard Rock

Glam Rock

Heavy Metal

Arena Rock

AOR Rock

Punk Rock

Grunge Rock

Indie Rock

Brit pop

Nu Metal

Garage Rock

Example 05 Riff

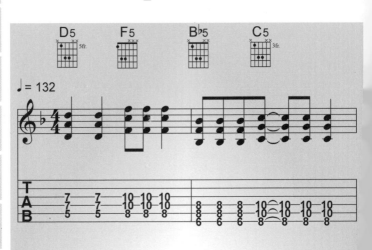

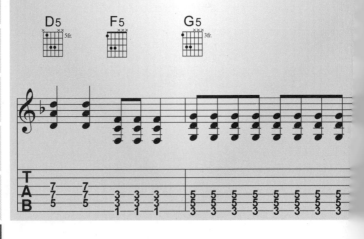

Garage Rock

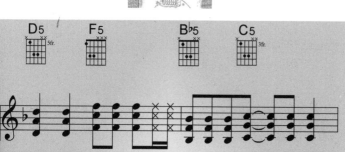

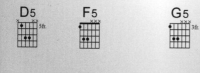

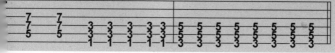

Blues Rock

Hard Rock

Glam Rock

Heavy Metal

Arena Rock

AOR Rock

Punk Rock

Grunge Rock

Indie Rock

Brit pop

Nu Metal

Garage Rock

Example 06 Riff

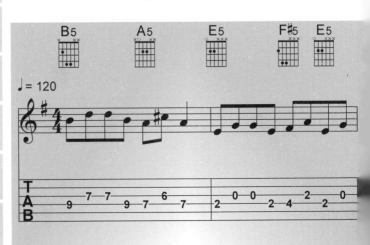

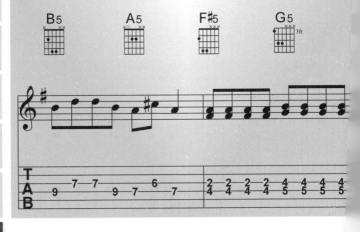

Garage Rock

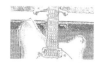

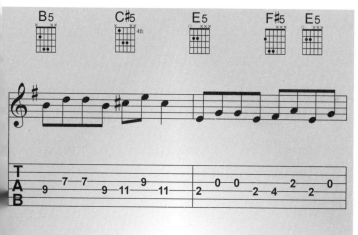

Blues
Rock

Hard
Rock

Glam
Rock

Heavy
Metal

Arena
Rock

AOR
Rock

Punk
Rock

Grunge
Rock

Indie
Rock

Brit
pop

Nu
Metal

Garage
Rock

Example 07 Riff

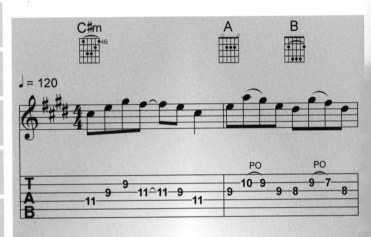

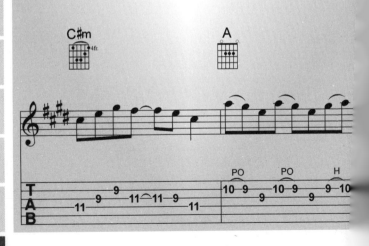

Garage Rock

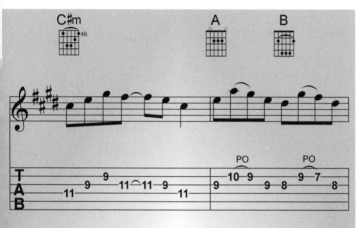

Blues Rock

Hard Rock

Glam Rock

Heavy Metal

Arena Rock

AOR Rock

Punk Rock

Grunge Rock

Indie Rock

Brit pop

Nu Metal

Garage Rock

Example 08 Riff

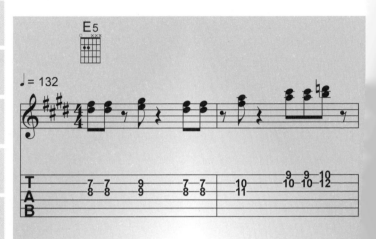

Blues
Rock

Hard
Rock

Glam
Rock

Heavy
Metal

Arena
Rock

AOR
Rock

Punk
Rock

Grunge
Rock

Indie
Rock

Brit
pop

Nu
Metal

Garage
Rock

Example 09 Lead

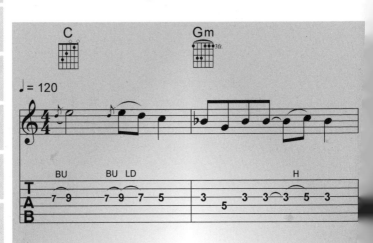

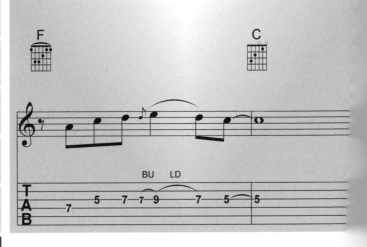

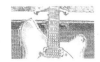

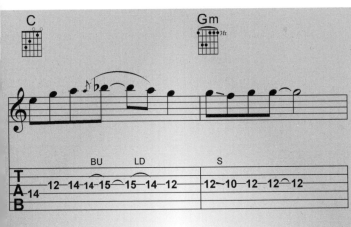

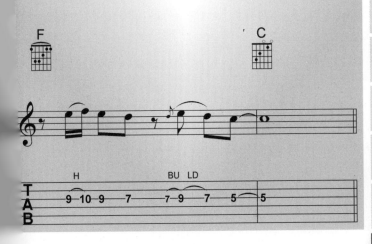

Blues
Rock

Hard
Rock

Glam
Rock

Heavy
Metal

Arena
Rock

AOR
Rock

Punk
Rock

Grunge
Rock

Indie
Rock

Brit
pop

Nu
Metal

Garage
Rock

Example 10 Lead

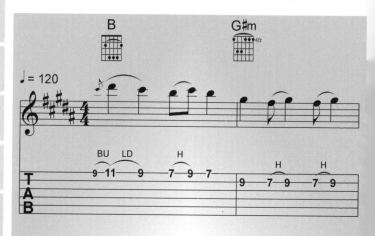

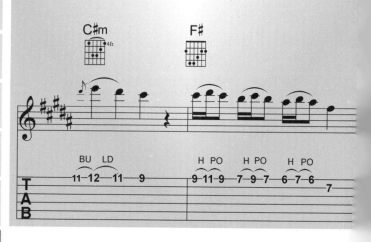

362

Garage Rock

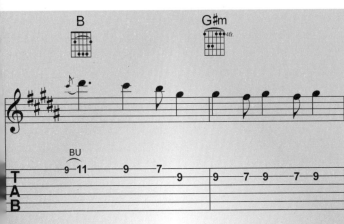

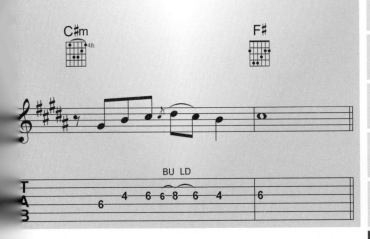

Blues Rock

Hard Rock

Glam Rock

Heavy Metal

Arena Rock

AOR Rock

Punk Rock

Grunge Rock

Indie Rock

Brit pop

Nu Metal

Garage Rock

Example 11 Lead

Blues Rock
Hard Rock
Glam Rock
Heavy Metal
Arena Rock
AOR Rock
Punk Rock
Grunge Rock
Indie Rock
Brit pop
Nu Metal
Garage Rock

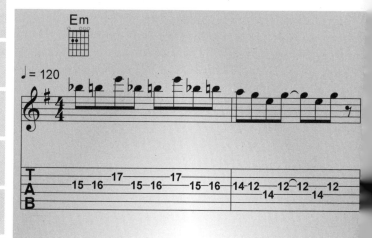

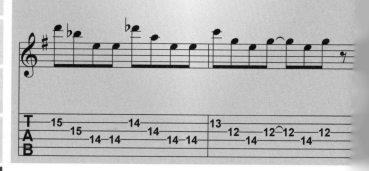

Garage Rock

Blues Rock

Hard Rock

Glam Rock

Heavy Metal

Arena Rock

AOR Rock

Punk Rock

Grunge Rock

Indie Rock

Brit pop

Nu Metal

Garage Rock

Example 12 Lead

Blues
Rock

Hard
Rock

Glam
Rock

Heavy
Metal

Arena
Rock

AOR
Rock

Punk
Rock

Grunge
Rock

Indie
Rock

Brit
pop

Nu
Metal

Garage
Rock

Garage Rock

Blues Rock

Hard Rock

Glam Rock

Heavy Metal

Arena Rock

AOR Rock

Punk Rock

Grunge Rock

Indie Rock

Brit pop

Nu Metal

Garage Rock

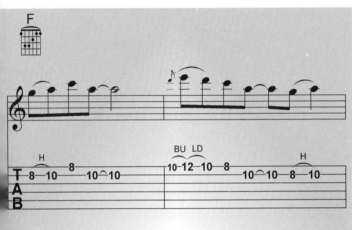

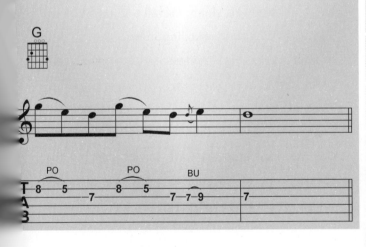

A Short History of Rock

The Sixties

The origins of Sixties rock were firmly rooted in the blues – yet it was ironic that the music that emanated from the oppressed black South of the United States was developing faster in Britain. Acts like the Yardbirds, John Mayall's Bluesbreakers, Fleetwood Mac and the Rolling Stones returned it to its land of origin with interest and with real success.

The Kinks have been credited with creating the first heavy metal record in the shape of 1964's 'You Really Got Me', lead guitarist Dave Davies slashing the speaker cone of his amp to get a raw, distorted sound. American garage rockers like the Shadows of

The Rolling Stones

Knight, the Kingsmen and the Seeds developed this. Also from British pop roots came George Harrison – admittedly one of the lesser-heralded Beatles, but one whose understated guitar style and slide work was influential on a generation.

As musicians became well known in their own right, something only singers had previously enjoyed, the concept of a supergroup arose – putting great talents together. This path was followed by Cream who, by introducing drug-induced psychedelia into the mix, created a much-copied formula that critics claimed allowed bands and guitarists to solo at will as long as the musicians began and ended the song at the same time. But the three bandleader-sized egos would only co-exist for less than three years, profitable and creative years though they were.

A folk-rock strand began with the Byrds, whose sound was based around the 12-string Rickenbacker guitar of Roger McGuinn. This proved a recurring theme through the following decades with artists as diverse as Tom Petty and the Stone Roses both appropriating the sound and doing radically different things with it.

Jimi Hendrix was the one man who expanded the possibilities of rock guitar more than any other. His wild, expressive playing, mistreatment of his instrument and use of effects would reverberate long after his unfortunate and premature death in 1970. The hard-edged blues of Ten Years After (featuring Woodstock hero Alvin Lee) and Free proved easier to imitate. Strong echoes of their work would be heard in the music of Lynyrd Skynyrd and the Black Crowes, while Mexico's Carlos Santana came from south of the border to not only impress the Woodstock festival crowd, but also his contemporaries by patenting a smooth, legato playing style millions still hear and enjoy today.

The Seventies

If the Sixties was the emotion of the blues expressed through guitar-playing, the Seventies saw virtuosity take centre stage. Effects also began to alter the sound of the guitar, moving from the relatively simple wah-wah and octave divider as pioneered by Hendrix to altogether more complex phasing, flanging, delay and more. As rock lost direction, many guitarists were accused of using effects as a substitute for innovation.

Glam was pop's answer to this seriousness, and bands like Slade, Sweet, Mud and even Queen (who successfully straddled rock and pop, albeit for a short while) applied rock guitar to chart-worthy songs in an admirably direct fashion. They didn't forget that the idea was to appeal further than fellow musicians. T. Rex, led by Marc Bolan,

Jimmy Page of Led Zeppelin

electrified folk by adding Eddie Cochran-style retro guitar riffs to snappy new songs. Like Queen, however, these soon became overproduced and repetitive – an accusation that could be levelled at much guitar rock of the era.

The idea of twin lead guitars gained currency through bands like Wishbone Ash, Thin Lizzy and, in America, the Allman Brothers Band. Outstanding stylists like Ritchie Blackmore (Deep Purple/Rainbow), Paul Kossoff (Free/Backstreet Crawler) and Eddie Clarke (Motörhead) continued to impress, though sadly Kossoff's creative spark was lost to drugs. Kiss, Lynyrd Skynyrd and Judas Priest all also started up successful franchises.

Led Zeppelin, Pink Floyd and King Crimson were bands whose heyday was the Seventies though they all started life in the Sixties. The music was complex, demanding and well beyond the capabilities of mere mortal guitarists. The world marvelled, but at a distance, as Jimmy Page, Dave Gilmour and Robert Fripp sent up their barrage of cultured chords and well-researched riffs. Genesis's Steve Hackett deserved a place at this top table but was somewhat overshadowed by both his rivals and other band members.

The arrival of punk changed things – simple music delivered at maximum volume with a guitar often plugged straight into the amplifier was the order of the day. One of the fanzines put it this way: 'Here's one chord, here's another and another. Now form a band.' More people picked up the guitar than at any time since the swinging Sixties, and the effect was more than welcome.

The States never quite bought into punk, and at the end of the decade, the emergence of Van Halen showed that heavy rock had life yet. Leader Eddie Van Halen, 'an acrobat of hammering chords, exhausting vibratos, melodic riffs and Hendrix-ian glissandos' according to one critic, brought virtuosity back into fashion.

The Eighties

If Eddie Van Halen had prepared the ground for an Eighties guitar revival, then two men, Steve Vai and his teacher Joe Satriani, were responsible for taking hold of the torch and igniting the rock scene. Their style – extremely fast, flowing and technical –became known as shredding. Symphonic and classical elements were explored by the likes of Uli Jon Roth and Yngwie Malmsteen, from Germany and Sweden respectively, proving that guitar innovation now came from all points of the compass. The iconic guitar of the day was the

Iron Maiden

Ibanez with its pointed headstock and locking Floyd Rose tremolo system.

The commercially popular guitar-based rock of bands like Bon Jovi, Def Leppard and Aerosmith harked back to the image-conscious glam wave of the Seventies and contrasted with the darker black metal of Venom. A new wave of British heavy metal emerged in the early Eighties that would spawn the likes of Iron Maiden, Saxon and Def Leppard. Maiden proved influential in introducing mythology and legend into their music. Bluesman Stevie Ray Vaughan blazed brightly but briefly. Yet if one single guitarist bestrode the decade it was U2's the Edge (real name Dave Evans), whose waves of effects-laden sound, picked up from the Police's Andy Summers, provided the foundation for not only Bono's equally impassioned vocal but the success of albums like *The Unforgettable Fire* (1984) and *The Joshua Tree* (1987).

The Nineties

Riding in on a twin wave of Metallica and Guns N'Roses, both of whom would sell many millions of records, the Nineties would turn out to be a more varied decade than its predecessor. It saw the rise and fall of grunge, where lyrics were secondary to the quiet verse-loud chorus formula of bands like Nirvana, Soundgarden and Pearl Jam. In a throwback to punk, Nirvana's Kurt Cobain played entry-level Fender Mustang guitars before being persuaded to design his own Mustang-Jaguar hybrid. Cobain was said to have 'killed the guitar solo', in a similar way to punk.

The Red Hot Chili Peppers were the most successful of a number of bands like Faith No More, Rage Against The Machine and Fishbone who mixed guitar rock with funk styles in a hark back to Hendrix. In Britain, bands like Blur and Oasis also had a retro bias, mixing old and new styles to create Britpop. The new Kinks and Beatles? Perhaps, but Syd Barrett's Pink Floyd and new wavers Wire were very much in Blur man Graham Coxon's thoughts.

Blur's lo-fi lead would be very much picked up by Radiohead, a highly influential guitar band whose Jonny Greenwood and Ed O'Brien would be the focus of attention for six-stringers as the band established itself as the decade's 'new Pink Floyd'. In the States, complexity was the name of the game as bands like Dream Theater reintroduced the long-derided concept of progression to rock music. Guitarist John Petrucci found he needed a seven-string axe to keep up.

Yet there was still room for basic guitar rock, as Green Day proved when they became the major success of Woodstock's 25th anniversary re-run. Billie Joe Armstrong was no Hendrix, but the Grammy-winning performance of 1994's *Dookie* made them the darlings of the MTV set – they picked up nine award nominations from the channel.

While speed and thrash metal lost some impetus, as their proponents diversified into more specific genres or followed Metallica into the rock

Nirvana drummer turned Foo Fighters frontman Dave Grohl.

mainstream, a wave of black metal from Scandinavia hit the headlines with a series of deaths, murders and church-burnings. Norwegian bands such as Burzum, Satyricon, Immortal, Enslaved and Emperor found themselves embroiled in this controversy.

As the Nineties ended, nu metal bands like Limp Bizkit, Korn and Papa Roach made a successful bid for the airwaves with their blend of rock and rap. Rock was alive and well.

The Noughties

With a revived Green Day leading the way, a back-to-basics garage rock revival hit the Noughties with bands like the White Stripes, the Strokes, the Vines and the Hives all battering down the door to the charts with successful singles and albums. Britain responded with the Libertines, Bloc Party and Franz Ferdinand. In contrast to these low-key outfits, a wave of emo (emotional) bands including My Chemical Romance, Fall Out Boy and Panic! At The Disco finally brought to the mainstream a strand of music that originated in Washington DC as far back as the mid-Eighties.

Nu metal peaked early in the decade with the success of Limp Bizkit's *Chocolate Starfish And The Hot Dog Flavored Water* (2000). But as the decade wore on, Guns N'Roses spinoff Velvet Revolver, Stone Sour and even more extreme bands like Trivium and Machine Head seemed to be taking their places at the top table. Nirvana's Dave Grohl also made a credible bid for world domination by switching from drums to guitar and fronting Foo Fighters, arguably the group of the first half of the decade. Muse were the most promising British band to challenge for honours, guitarist Matt Bellamy the son of a Sixties guitar hero from the Tornados.

Further Reading

Heatley, M. (ed), *The Definitive Illustrated Encyclopedia of Rock*, Flame Tree Publishing, 2006; Heatley, M., *How to Play Hard, Metal & Nu Rock*, Flame Tree Publishing, 2008; Heatley, M., *How to Write Great Songs*, Flame Tree Publishing, 2007; Jackson, J. (ed), *Guitar Chords*, Flame Tree Publishing, 2006; Johnston, R., *How to Play Rock Guitar: The Basics and Beyond*, Backbeat Books, 2003; Leonard, M. (ed), *The Illustrated Complete Guitar Handbook*, Flame Tree Publishing, 2005; Skinner, T., *Playing Techniques: 10 Easy-to-Follow Guitar Lessons*, Registry Publications Ltd, 2006; Skinner, T., *Rock and Metal: 10 Easy-to-Follow Guitar Lessons*, Registry Publications Ltd, 2006; Skinner, T. and Drudy, A., *Blues and Rock: 10 Easy-to-Follow Guitar Lessons*, Registry Publications Ltd, 2006; Sokolow, F., *Fretboard Roadmaps: Rock Guitar*, Music Sales Ltd, 2001; Stetina, T., *Speed Mechanics for Lead Guitar*, Music Sales Ltd, 1992; Stetina, T., *Total Rock Guitar: A Complete Guide to Learning Rock Guitar*, Hal Leonard Publishing Corporation, 2001; Wolfshon, M.P., *The Ultimate Rock Guitar Scale Finder*, Hal Leonard Publishing Corporation, 2007.

Internet Sites

www.accessrock.com: interactive website with free guitar lessons, tips and advice from experts; *www.guitarknowledgenet.com*: large collection of tools and lessons for guitarists of all abilities; *www.guitarmasterclass.net*: free daily video lessons with tabs and a guitar forum; *www.guitarsolos.com*: guitar tablature archive with interactive and video solos and riffs; *www.guitarworld.com*: online guitar magazine with news, lessons, video interviews and tabs; *www.kerrang.com*: online rock magazine with news, features, interviews and podcasts.